SECULARISM—CONCEPT AND PRACTICE

About the Author

Dr. A.K. Lal is a well known sociologist from Bihar having three decades of experience in research and training. Dr. Lal has worked on different things and has successfully completed projects funded by the Central Government as well as Voluntary Organization. He has special interests in the problems of *dalits* which finds articulation in his contributions facilitating understanding of the phenomenon of change and continuity among these people. He has long experience of field work in Bihar, Haryana, Madhya Pradesh and Delhi. Dr. Lal has been in close rapport with Sociological activities of Sulabh International and has been founder Director of its institutions for research and social intervention. During his stay in Sulabh International he organised courses for sanitation and rural development and helped the organization in initiating programmes for upliftment and social integration of scavengers. Dr. Lal has authored a number of books including the well known work on Bonded Labours in Bihar entitled *Politics and Poverty*. His other books are *The Urban Family, Elite and Development* (with Sachchidananda) and *Harijan Elite* (with Sachchidananda), and *Dalits in Action*. In addition to these he has written a number of research articles and book reviews. Dr. Lal is presently a senior fellow in the G. B. Pant Social Science Institute Allahabad.

SECULARISM
CONCEPT AND PRACTICE

Editor
A. K. LAL
G. B. Pant Social Science Institute, Allahabad

CONCEPT PUBLISHING COMPANY, NEW DELHI 110059

ISBN 81-7022-729-1

First Published 1998

Published and Printed by
Ashok Kumar Mittal
Concept Publishing Company
A/15-16, Commercial Block, Mohan Garden
New Delhi 110059 (India)

Phones: 5649024, 5648039
Fax: 091–(11)–5648053

Dedicated to the sacred memory of
my respected father
Shri Shivanandan Lal, a karmayogi.

PREFACE

India has been a land of religious tolerance. Peaceful co-existence has been its ideal. Plurality has been the essential feature of Indian social order. Secularism has been an ideology of its people. We still remain wedded to diversity in spite of excessive polarisation. Secularism, however, needs to be kept in firm rapport with the orientation and the behaviour of the people. It has to be nurtured to tide over avoidable complexities, threatening to rupture its social texture. In a society like India, secularism has to be a strategy for peace and harmony. Our commitment to the ideology of secularism has to be strengthened specially in the context of continuing onslaught of the forces of fundamentalism. There is a need for continuous dialogue on the problem of communalism that exists in spite of sincere attempts to root it out.

It was with this intent that a seminar on "Secularism—Concept and Practice" was held at A.N. Sinha Institute of Social Studies, Patna in November 1993 in collaboration with the Indian Social Institute, New Delhi. The response to our invitation to participate in the seminar was overwhelming. The deliberations were highly fruitful. Among those who participated in the discussion included distinguished social activists, eminent sociologists, well-known political scientists and leading journalists. While different dimensions of the phenomenon were discussed, the seminar did not aim at unanimity of opinion. The present work includes the papers presented in the seminar. It also includes papers specially written on the theme after the conclusion of the seminar.

I am obliged to the authors who contributed articles of exceptionally high quality for inclusion in the volume. These are likely to provide adequate understanding of the phenomenon of secularism, specially in the context of Bihar. I am grateful to Dr. Sebasti L. Raj, the Executive Director of the Indian Social Institute for inspiring me to do this work. He also provided the needed financial support for the seminar.

Shri M.J. Phillip, Shri Ram Ikbal Das and Shri Jitendra Pandey deserve my thanks for their help in typing the manuscript. Shri Dipak Kumar Sinha, an experienced member of my research team, provided me his enthusiastic support at every stage. He deserves special thanks. I am appreciative of the help provided by my family members, specially my daughter Suprabha and son Anurag in preparing this volume. The present work is dedicated to my father Shri Shiv Nandan Lal—a *Karmayogi*,—who remains a source of inspiration to me even after his death.

A.K. LAL

OUR CONTRIBUTORS

1. *Shri S.K. Sinha* — Governor of Assam
2. *Dr. Bindeshwar Pathak* — Founder, Sulabh Movement
3. *Acharya Rama Murti* — Noted Gandhian, thinker and social activist
4. *Prof. Ali Ashraf* — Former Director, Gandhian Institute of Studies, Varanasi
5. *Prof. A.K. Lal* — Senior Fellow, G. B. Pant Social Science Institute, Allahabad
6. *Prof. B.P. Sinha* — Reitred Prof. of Ancient Indian History, Patna University, Patna
7. *Dr. Jose Kananaikil* — Action Sociologist, Director, Bihar Dalit Vikas Samiti
8. *Dr. R.P. Sinha* -- Reader in Sociology, A.N. Sinha Institute of Social Studies, Patna
9. *Dr. Vijay Kumar* — Reader in Political Science, S.K. Bhagalpur University
10. *Dr. Jitendra Narayan* — Reader in Political Science, L.N. Mithila University, Darbhanga
11. *Dr. Nil Ratan* — Reader in Political Science, A.N. Sinha Institute of Social Studies, Patna
12. *Dr. R.K. Verma* — Research Fellow, Jagjivan Ram Institute of Parliamentary Studies and Political Research, Patna

13. *Dr. Suresh Prasad* — Research Officer, A.N. Sinha Institute of Social Studies, Patna

14. *Dr. Harshvardhan* — Department of Political Science, L.N. Mithila University, Darbhanga

CONTENTS

1

INTRODUCTION

A. K. Lal

Secularism has been defined and interpreted in different ways. It has many meanings and lacks conceptual clarity. Ambiguity shrouds its formulation. It implies a wide variety of phenomenon "containing within it a host of alternative ideological possibilities."[1] The term emerged in the context of medieval struggle between the church and the state. In this sense it is the intellectual child of the western renaissance.[2] Its origin, therefore, tends to be 'ethno-centric in context and reference'.[3] Its initial intent was to separate the church from the state. In order to find a solution to the bitter and protracted conflict between the two the properties of the church were taken by the state leaving the former confined to the task of catering to the transcendent other-worldly and spiritual needs of the people. "What was a matter of fact statement then become later after the French Revolution a value statement".[4] In its broad formulation, secularism represents an outline of society which modernization seeks to attain. In this sense it refers to a process that aims to inaugurate a functional differentiation of the social order leading to the weakening of the stratified differentiation of the traditional society.[5] While it seeks to question the supremacy of the ascriptive categories in the society as the overriding principle of its organization its specific concern has been to rid the society from the evils of excessive religiosity. In this sense secularization refers to a situation characterised by separation of state from religion. It is intended to provide redemption from the fetters of religion. Secularization is conceived as a process "in which religion loses its hold on the level of both institution and of human consciousness".[6] It is the process by which sections of society and culture are removed from the domination of religious institutions and symbols. It implies an attitude to life and a commitment to a set of values which can be described as secular as opposed to supernatural.

Secularism in other words is a mode of orientation to the phenomenal world which is indifferent to or actively rejects traditional religious orientations in preference for exclusively humanist this worldly orientations. Secularism emphasises break with religious outlook. In these formulations religion is taken to be an aberration and a hangover from the traditional past. Religion loses its strength in the wake of instrumental rationality of the modernising present. It exists as a painful survival of the past that is capable of being erased in the wake of economic development and scientific progress.

Secularism is a familiar concept in India. It is deeply entrenched in Indian academic, political and legal discourse. It is not a simple intellectual abstraction, but rather a sheet anchor of the state policy. It is an ideology as well as a praxis. It is an effective philosophy to shape the value premises and interactional matrices of the people in India. It constitutes a phenomenon of perspective importance. Secularism is a distinct feature of India's cultural heritage and is suited to the complexities of the prevalent reality. Indian secularism is premised on transcendent unity of ultimate reality. Tolerant pluralism is its essence. It favours equal appreciation of all religions. The provision for freedom of conscience as enshrined in the Constitution of India is wedded to the ideal of nurturing the instincts of togetherness without questioning the peculiarities in its diversity. India's model of secularism approximates to the nondiscriminatory model where the state accords equal treatment to all religions. It implies religious pluralism. It does not aim at the removal of religion from the society. "India is a secular state in the sense that tolerance and respect for religious pluralism (are) encouraged by the state because different faiths represent different paths to the same absolute and universal truth... The secular state encourages tolerance and religious pluralism not because of its neutrality on matters of religious nature but because of an assumed religious orientation toward truth and equality."[7] The fundamental ingredients of Indian composite culture have their deep imprint in the official ideology for nation building. In a society with complex social organization encouragement to religious pluralism is possible through secularism. Secularism seeks to promote integration without disturbing the diversity. Its praxis is intended to promote civil instincts in a setting riven by primordial cleavages and excessive traditionalism. Unity in diversity has to be achieved through the efforts leading to the weaving of heterogeneous in a cohesive framework. "It is an ideology to usher a guided transition of a traditional society into a modern polity by emphasising certain values and norms of civil life and political culture." [8] Secularism is an aspiration for the supremacy of the state and rationality of its people.

Secularism as being practised in India has been subjected to criticisms. Its prevalent conceptualization and consequent implications tend to be questioned. Indian secularism has been criticised for its failure to contain religious stresses and strains. It is considered to be an ideology of the state. It has failed to be an effective reference model to guide the shaping of social interaction in the society. As such it remains statist. It has undergone excessive politicization. It has not gone deep in the domain of civil society. It is also said to have been used more for the partisan and selfish purpose of securing political mileage than to seek adherence to its original agenda. Obscurantist customs and practices tend to find support in the name of religious neutrality. "That the state intervened to quell communal riots though not always promptly, impartially and decisively is not an expression of its secular commitment but an effort to maintain law and order necessary for effective administration".[9] Nandy[10] finds its adaptation in India a surrender to the forces of academic imperialism of the west oriented to the task of promotion of western science and rationality. He finds it to be alien to moral tradition of Indian society and least effective as a mechanism to ensure harmony and mutuality. Srinivas[11] pleads for rejection of mainstream secularism as he feels it to be oriented to individualistic and amoral social order incompatible with the organic, harmonious and holistic structure of traditional India. Secularism is considered to be a foreign import and an imposition on the society by its modernizing elite. Madan[12] feels that "in the prevailing circumstances secularism in South Asia as a generally shared creed of life is impossible, as a basis of state action impracticable and as a blue print for the foreseeable future impotent." Indian secularism is also criticised for its insincere and selective application. The gap between aspiration and practical implementation seems to be wide. In the papers that have been included here there is an attempt to initiate fresh dialogue on the concept and practice of secularism in India.

Lt. General (Retd.) S.K. Sinha analyses the phenomenon of communalism in India in the historical perspective. He tries to isolate factors contributing to decline of secularism in the post-Nehruvian period. He feels that factors contributing the growth of communalism have to be contained. Proper orientation and effective leadership has to be harnessed. In his opinion secularism is an inescapable imperative for a pluralistic society and it has to be preserved.

Padma Bhushan Dr. Bindeshwar Pathak talks of resilience characterising the Indian society. Its basic features continue in spite of the operation of forces of modernization. Ethnic diversity and cultural heterogeneity perpetuates itself in Indian society since time immemorial. He blames politics for division of society on communal lines. There is a need for the people to turn inward to seek spiritual guidance to promote social integration. Dr. Pathak regards secularism to be an alien concept not suited to the genius of the Indian society.

Prof. Ali Ashraf pleads for an analysis of the socio-economic correlates of communalism. This he feels necessary for understanding the phenomenon of secularism in its totality.

Prof. A.K. Lal analyses the concept and practice of communalism in India. He makes an attempt to isolate the reasons for communal flare-up. In addition he elaborates the social composition of participants in the riots, nature of riot-affected areas and many more things related to it.

Sri Acharya Rama Murti expresses the predicament of a Gandhian in society frequently disturbed by communalism. As an effective interventionalist, he elaborates his personal experiences of encounters in riot situations.

Dr. Vijay Kumar criticises secularism as its practice has led to protectionalism in Indian society. According to him it represents an aspiration of the minorities who want to shape the majority in their own image.

Dr. J. Narayan analyses the communal incidents in Bihar to identify the essential features of riots. His paper has special for us on efficacy of administration in situations causing communal flare-ups.

Dr. R.K. Verma touches upon the problem of religious fanaticism. Secularism remains exclusive in the absence of an egalitarian opportunity structure. Dr. Verma is of the opinion that effective intervention by a sincere political leadership helps in maintaining communal peace and harmony.

Dr. Harshvardhan criticises the exploitation of issues of secularism by politicians. This tends to perpetuate communal divide. It also keeps the people in a state of perpetual backwardness. He pleads for right interpretation of the ideology of secularism, so that its intents are achieved.

Dr. R.P. Sinha's paper is guided by the belief that the system of formal education is *NOT* always secular in content and form. Deriving its argument from historical realities, the paper examines development of formal education in India since MacCaulay, through the post-Independence era and holds that English system of formal education in India was essentially a mechanism of proselytisation. Dr. Sinha argues that given this situation in which even Constitution fosters protective discrimination, the system of formal education will continue to be non-secular unless it is replaced by scientific and moral education in which religion has no place.

Prof. A.K. Lal maintains that compensation for loss of traditional bases of support has led the embeded to arrange strength for their dominance through false and insincere initiatives to lift the dalits in the traditional Hindu stratification system. Prof. Lal has culled out evidences in support of his thesis from different parts of the country.

Dr. Nil Ratan examines the predicament of common civil code in Indian society. He subjects legal provisions in this regard to close scrutiny.

Dr. Suresh Prasad makes a plea for concerted attempts aimed at destruction of communalism. Secularism does not survive in a communal setting. He is of the opinion that the philosophical foundation sustaining communalism has to be destroyed in order to promote national integration.

Dr. Jose Kananaikil considers pluralism to be the essence of society. He analyses the power structure of the Indian society, with the help of the concepts of centre and periphery. He feels that the power structure of the Indian society is in a state of flux. The traditionally deprived have to federate themselves to stake for equality in socio-economic relations.

Prof. B. P. Sinha considers the stresses and strains afflicting the task of national integration to be a spill-over from our historical past. He finds lessons of Indian history to be relevant in guiding the people and the state in maintaining harmony and stability. He pleads for emulation of the model of concord adopted by Ashoka.

REFERENCES

1. Dipankar Gupta, 'Secularism and Minoritisation'. *Economic and Political Weekly,* Vol. 30, No. 35, Sept. 1995, p. 2203.
2. P.C. Joshi, *Secularism and Development,* Vikas Publishing House Pvt. Ltd., New Delhi, 1995.
3. Rasheeduddin Khan, *Bewildered India,* Har-Anand Publications, New Delhi, 1994, p. 276.
4. T. N. Madan, 'Secularism in its place' in *Religion in India,* Oxford University Press, New Delhi, 1991, p. 394.
5. Niklas Lumman, *The Differentiation of Society,* Columbia University Press, New York, 1982.
6. Peter Berger, *The Sacred Canopy: Elements of Sociological Theory of Religion,* Doubleday Garden City, 1970.
7. Douglas Allen, 'Introduction' to *Religion and Political Conflict in South Asia,* Oxford University Press, Bombay, 1993, p. 8.
8. Rasheeduddin Khan, *op. cit.*
9. K.N. Pannikar, 'Introduction' to *Communalism in India,* Manohar, Delhi, 1991, p. 11.
10. Ashish Nandy, 'An Anti-Secularist Manifesto', *Seminar,* October 1985.
11. M.N. Srinivas, *Times of India,* 1993.
12. T.N. Madan, *op. cit.*

2

CONCEPT AND PRACTICE OF SECULARISM

S.K. Sinha

Introduction

Our Independence movement was profoundly secular but secularism as a word did not figure in the political vocabulary of that struggle. Our founding fathers gave us a very secular Constitution yet secularism as a word did not figure in it. It was later incorporated in the preamble to the Constitution through an amendment in 1976. Ironically, after this amendment, politics in India started getting increasingly less secular. Today secularism is the most oft-repeated word by our politicians but it is least practised by them.

Concept of Secularism

There is confusion regarding the real meaning of secularism. The accepted Hindi translation of this word, *Dharmanirpeksha* (religious neutrality), does not convey the real meaning of the word. Secularism is something more positive than just religious neutrality. One needs to go into the history of secularism to appreciate its nuances and the variance between Western and Indian concepts of secularism.

Secularism in the West was a product of the Age of Reason. Machiavelli (1469-1527) first mooted the idea of a secular state, free from ecclesiastical interference. During the medieval period, the Church in Europe was very powerful. It was a supranational power, more powerful than the state. It had vast resources at its disposal. Thirty per cent of the agricultural land in Europe was owned by the Church and at that time agriculture was the mainstay of economy. The people were steeped in ignorance and superstition. Henry VIII of England raised the standard of revolt against the Church, when the Pope denied him permission to marry his brother's widow. Disowning allegiance to the Church of Rome, he started his own Church, the Church of England and assumed the title of the Defender of the faith. The British Sovereign continues to have this title to this day. Concurrently, Protestantism started spreading rapidly all over Europe except France, Spain and Italy, which continued to remain Catholic. The political authority of the Pope got greatly weakened. This was dramatically demonstrated during the coronation of Napoleon. The Pope had been invited to Paris for this function but when the time came for His Holiness to consecrate the crown and place it on Napoleon's head, Napoleon picked up the crown himself and put it on, saying, "The crown of France was lying in the gutter from where I picked it up." This dramatic incident in Catholic France symbolised the independence of the State from the Church. The dictionary meaning of secularism conforms to this concept, emphasising the separation of politics from religion. With the rise of communism, a new twist was given to the meaning of secularism. Marx and Lenin propounded that religion was the opium of the masses. The Communist State became anti-religion.

Secularism, as practised in the West and avidly adopted by the Westernised sections of our people, is alien to the Indian ethos. India's secular tradition is not only much older but it is also unique and very different from that of the West. Ashoka's Rock Edict No. 12 dating back to the third century B.C. proclaimed that the Emperor treated all his subjects as his children and wanted all religions to be given due respect. People of different faiths coming to India at different periods of our history found asylum in this country and were given full freedom to practise their religion. Inquisition, crusade or *Jehad* was something foreign to Indian thinking and was not indulged in by Indians. The disciples of Christ brought Christianity to India soon after His crucifixion and before that religions had travelled to Europe. Christianity was allowed to flourish in India without any hindrance at a time when Christians were being barbarously persecuted in Rome. Jews fleeing from Roman tyranny during the Diaspora of 70 A.D. were given refuge in India. Some of the Jewish synagogues in Kerala are of ancient origin. Zoroastrians, forced to abandon their country after the rise of Islam in the seventh century A.D., were also given asylum in India. Today, the Parsis are one of our most progressive communities, who have been making commendable contribution in every sphere of our national activity. Islam came to India as the religion of Muslim conquerors. They plundered the people and razed thousands of Hindu temples to the ground. Some bigoted Muslim rulers persecuted the Hindus. Yet there was no retaliation from the Hindus. Hindu military renaissance led by Shivaji may have been against Muslim rulers but was not anti-Islam. In fact he was known to have always gone out of his way to show respect for mosques and for copies of the Holy Book that fell in his hands. He was both generous and reverential towards Muslim saints who were given grants. Kufi Khan, a contemporary historian who was highly critical of Shivaji, praised him for his respectful attitude towards Islam. The Sufi tradition blended with Bhakti cult and gained widespread acceptance in India. The two communities learnt to co-exist amicably and developed a composite culture. At the World Parliament of Religions in Chicago, Swami Vivekanand expounding the Vedantic philosophy argued that religious tolerance was not enough, there should be religious acceptance. Religions were different paths leading to the same infinite Lord and there should be no conflict between them. Thus the Indian tradition has been of religious harmony and acceptance. Separation of religion and politics as practised in the West is contrary to the Indian ethos.

Our Independence struggle was secular but it drew heavily upon religion. Bal Gangadhar Tilak gave a political colour to Ganpati Puja. He wrote a commentary on the *Geeta* and so did Mahatma Gandhi and C. Rajagopalachari. The Mahatma freely mixed religion with politics. His prayer meetings at which he made political speeches used to start with the reading of extracts from the holy books of all religions and with the singing of hymns of different faiths. Maulana Abul Kalam Azad and Maulana Mazharul Haque were deeply religious but at the same time they were ardent practitioners of secular politics. Maulana Azad's speeches and writings used to invariably start with quotations from the *Koran*. Nehru, however, was an agnostic and his secularism had a pronounced western tilt.

Having discussed the history of secularism in the West and in India, we may now examine what secularism really means. Secularism is not against religion, but it is against religious disharmony and strife. It is the antithesis of communalism. It is more "Sarva Dharma Sambhava" (all religions are equal) than "Dharmanirpeksh" (religious neutrality). A good way to view it is in terms of three relationships — the relationship between the individual and religion, between the individual and the State, and between the State and religion. The State should not interfere in the first, religion should not interfere in the second and so far as the third is concerned, the State should treat all religions alike. The requirement is not so much to separate religion from politics as to prevent misuse of religion in politics.

Practice of Secularism

Despite our long and liberal traditions, the twentieth century has witnessed the phenomenal growth of communalism in India. In the first wave a crescendo was reached in 1947 and in the second wave in 1992 from where it does not appear to be receding. These waves have been caused by the play of politics of power against the combustible backdrop of separate identity, mass ignorance and misleading notions of history. Before discussing how the politics of power has been played, it is necessary to examine each of the three aspects constituting the backdrop.

The rapid spread of Islam from Spain to Indonesia was a unique phenomenon of world history. There was wholesale conversion to Islam in most countries coming under Muslim rule. The entire people of Egypt, Iran, Malaysia, Indonesia minus the small island of Bali and so on, embraced the new religion discarding their previous religion. India was one of the few countries where this did not happen. Despite centuries of Muslim rule, Hinduism not only survived but remained the dominant religion of the country. Possibly, this was on account of the large population of India and the resilience of Hinduism. In the past the Hindu society had assimilated migrations into India as also the faith of the migrants. The question of this happening with Islam did not arise as it had its own fully developed culture and it was the religion of the new rulers of India. Moreover, the orthodoxy of the Hindu society and its social taboos ruled out any such possibility. The two religious communities have always had a marked separate identity. However, the two learnt to co-exist cordially, even participating in each other's religious festivals. The two even developed a composite culture but their separate identity persisted. In Indonesia and Iran, the entire population had embraced Islam. There was thus no compulsion to zealously guard any separate identity. The

Indonesian Muslims have no inhibitions in continuing with *Ramayan* and *Mahabharat* ballets which to this day are popular in that country. In Iran, the Shah used to be proud of his title of Aryamehr and he celebrated the 2500th anniversary of monarchy in his country with great fanfare, even though this event preceded the rise of Islam by nearly a millennium. This outlook has been missing among the Indian Muslims. Being a minority and to guard against being engulfed by a majority, they are more assertive about their separate identity and their attitude to India's pre-Islamic heritage is very different.

The masses, both Hindus and Muslims, are largely ignorant and illiterate. They are not fully aware of their own religion, leave alone knowing anything about another religion. They get more influenced by rituals and dogmas than the essence of their religion. The Hindu concept of "*Vasudhaiv Kutumbakam*" (entire humanity is one family) is matched by the Islamic concept of Allah being "Rabul-Alameen" (Lord of mankind) and not "Rabul-Musalmeen" (Lord of Muslims). Similarly, the Hindu belief of all religions leading to the Lord by different paths, finds echo in the *Koran*, which teaches tolerance of all religions. The *Koran* states, "And abuse not those whom they call upon besides *Allah* lest exceeding the limits, they abuse *Allah* through ignorance. Thus to evey people we have made their deeds fair-seeming." The ignorance of the masses has made it easy for unscrupulous religious and political leaders to exploit them for their vested interests, leading to the growth of communalism.

Misleading notions of history have also been contributing to the divide between the two communities. The misconception about the Hindus being the original people of this country and the Muslims being outsiders is not based on historical facts. The Muslims are as indigenous to this country as the Hindus, even though their religion may be of foreign origin. The ancestors of over 95% of Indian Muslims were Hindus and they are the descendants of converts. Most of the remaining 5% are connected with Hindus by blood. Jehangir was the son of a Hindu mother, Jinnah the grandson of a Hindu and Zulfikar Ali Bhutto's grandmother was a Hindu. There is nothing derogatory in being a convert or the descendant of a convert. If one accepts that a religion was started at a particular point of time and it did not exist earlier, then the followers of that religion have to be either a convert or the descendant of a convert. The reluctance to accept this reality has caused distortions in the outlook of Indian Muslims. They tend to identify themselves with the invaders who came here from Central Asia rather than their ancestors conquered by those invaders. This also may be due to a complex inherited from the medieval period when foreign Muslims, notably Mughals, Turks, Iranians and Afghans enjoyed a much higher political and social status than Hindustani Muslims. The repeated plundering invasions of Mahmud Gazni and his atrocities on the Hindus need not be given unduly religious tones. He razed numerous Hindu temples to the ground but that was more to take away the wealth stored in them than to satisfy any religious frenzy. During his invasions of Central and West Asia, he was equally cruel to the Muslim people of those countries. There were some invaders like Timur whose memoirs refer to the *Jehad* that he led into India during which after capturing Delhi, he massacred one lakh Hindus at Loni, a village near Delhi. There was also another invader like Nadir who had no illusions about any *Jehad*. During the massacre of Delhi ordered by him, Hindus and Muslims suffered alike at the hands of his merciless soldiers. Besides invaders there were many Muslim rulers in this country, some of whom were religious bigots who persecuted the Hindus and destroyed their temples and many others who were inspired by noble ideals and showed due consideration for their Hindu subjects. Aurangzeb epitomised rulers of the former category though now-a-days some people have been working overtime on the basis of some stray incidents and doubtful documents to prove that he was a great liberal ruler, who was not anti-Hindu. History is a science of truth and facts should not be distorted for ulterior motives. There were of course many rulers in the medieval era under whom there was marked amity and trust between the two communities and irrespective of their religious faith, all people under their rule could live with dignity. The secularism practised by Sher Shah, Akbar, Shivaji, Dara Shikoh, Tipu Sultan and Ranjit Singh was indeed commendable. Without distorting history, the correct interpretation of facts and viewing them in the right perspective will go a long way to remove numerous misconceptions.

Against this backdrop of separate identity, mass ignorance and misleading notions of history, the play of power politics has played havoc. Understandably the British as part of their imperial policy practised divide and rule. They gave encouragement to the apprehension among the Muslims arising from living as a minority in a Hindu majority democratic polity. The Muslims had been rulers in this country before the British and psychologically they found it difficult to reconcile themselves to a position where on the basis of numbers they may have the second position. The British political master-stroke was the introduction of separate electorate. This was designed to deepen the divide between the two communities. Simultaneously, Mahatma Gandhi committed a grave blunder in supporting the *Khilafat* movement, even though his intentions and objective were noble. The Sultan of Turkey was considered the modern Khalifa and was regarded as both the temporal and spiritual head of the Islamic world. After Turkey's defeat in the First World War, he was dethroned. Despite religious affinity, the Arabs resented Turkish colonial rule which had been autocratic. They rejoiced at becoming independent of Turkey. In Turkey itself the dethronement of the Sultan was welcomed due to the urge for freedom from orthodoxy. The success of the revolution of Kamal Ataturk proved this. Yet the Mullahs in India tried to identify the Sultan or the Khalifa with Islam and misled the Muslim masses. The Mahatma's support for this movement had good short-term effect in promoting Hindu Muslim unity but its long-term effects were very harmful. It set a precedent for the use of religious sentiments for political gains. Ironically, Jinnah who was then in the Congress had opposed the move to support the *Khilafat* movement, stressing that religion should not be mixed with politics : The other fall-out from this was to encourage the Muslims to look beyond the frontiers of India on religious grounds. Both separate electorate and the *Khilafat* movement sowed the seeds of the two-nation theory.

Communalism triumphed over secularism when the country got partitioned in 1947. The country's bifurcation was accompanied by the massacre of one million innocent people and the uprooting of ten million people from their homes. Jinnah had been the proponent of the two-nation theory but after the tragedy of partition, he tried to go back to his secular moorings. His opening address to the Pakistan Constituent Assembly made a forceful plea for secularism and ruled out the possibility of Pakistan becoming a theocratic State. Before his death and within a year of Pakistan coming into being, he had realised the folly of partition and he died a disillusioned man. After his death, Pakistan opted to be a theocratic State, while truncated India stuck to secularism.

A true secularist, Nehru was keen that Muslims should in no way be discriminated against in India. As a proof of this, Muslims were provided opportunities to rise to the highest positions in different spheres both at the Centre and in the States. Muslims have risen to be the President of India, Vice-President, Chief Justice of Supreme Court, Cabinet Ministers, Cabinet Secretary, Air Chief, C-in-C of Army Commands and so on. At the State level in Bihar, Muslims have held evey top appointment viz. Governor, Chief Minister, Chief Justice, Police Chief and so on. This is in sharp contrast to what has been happening in Pakistan, where Hindus are denied even minor appointments leave alone getting to any top position. They have to carry special coloured identity cards to emphasise that they are second class citizens. Besides there being no discrimination against Muslims in India over appointments in Government, special provisions have been made in the Constitution for minority institutions, giving them facilities not available to the institutions of the majority community. This was done because it was felt that whereas the minority needed those facilities , the majority could do without them.

Secularism flourished satisfactorily in India during the Nehruvian era and the scars of partition got healed. The bitterness between the two communities disappeared even though there were occasional communal riots on some local issues but these were of a minor nature and were easily contained. Certain developments in the post-Nehruvian era have led to a grave threat arising to the survival of secularism in this country. These need to be discussed.

As most of their leaders had gone over to Pakistan, the Muslims in India had become virtually leaderless. A sense of insecurity prevailed amongst them and a tendency grew for them to vote *en bloc* in elections. There was also a sense of guilt over their role in bringing about the partition of the country. A notable feature had been that the Muslims living in States which remained in India were more active in the movement for Pakistan than those in States which broke away to form Pakistan. With the economic clout provided by petro dollars to Islamic fundamentalists the world over and the memories of partition fading away there has been a marked growth of fundamentalism among both Muslims and Hindus. The nuances of this phenomenon among the Hindus will be discussed later. Nehru's concern for ensuring that Muslims should not be discriminated against degenerated to what is being called the pampering of Muslims. Without taking any concrete steps to help the Muslim community and resolve their problems, the State began to resort to a whole lot of gimmicks to pander to their sentiments. Whereas no *Iftar* parties at State expense were held during Nehruvian era, these have now become the order of the day. Ostensibly this is sought to be justified as a measure to promote communal amity but the real motivation behind it is to secure the Muslim vote bank. The propriety of a secular state holding such religious functions for only one religious community and not for any other, is of course highly questionable. The decision to declare Prophet Muhammad's birthday a national holiday when it is not a holiday in many Muslim countries including obscurantist Saudi Arabia, where he was born, is yet another example of such pandering. Today the Prophet's birthday is a compulsory national holiday in India but the birthdays of Lords Ram, Krishna and Shiva are optional national holidays. Yet another example of such pandering to Muslim sentiments was the revolting spectacle of secular India seeking membership of the Organisation of Islamic States at Rabaat and being rightly rebuffed. Other such instances can also be quoted. The point being made is that through such ill-conceived actions, the State has been encouraging both Muslims and Hindu fundamentalism. The Muslims realise the advantage inherent in maintaining the unity of the Muslim vote bank and the Hindus through a feeling of resentment are being encouraged to become fundamentalists.

The debased political leadership of the post-Nehruvian era has been finding it convenient to exploit sectarian sentiments for the sake of garnering votes. Thus we have now reached a situation that despite all their tall talk, all political parties in the country are communal and none is really secular. The Congress has been in coalition with an avowedly communal party in Kerala, the Muslim League. It has been a party to the creation of a Muslim majority district in Kerala and declaring Friday as a holiday for certain institutions in Kerala. It undermined the verdict of the apex court in the Shah Bano case to appease Muslim obscurantist forces. Despite being in power at the Centre for decades, it has failed to take any action towards implementing the Directive Principle in the Constitution about a common civil code. It allowed the unlocking of Babri Masjid and the performance of *Shilanyas* at Ayodhya to pamper to the sentiments of Hindu fundamentalists. Its election manifesto in Mizoram held out promise for establishing a Christian State. In Punjab through setting up Bhindranwale as a religious leader it tried to counter the political influence of the Akalis. The Congress brand of communalism in politics has been opportunistic in that its tilt has been varying from one community to another, to suit its perception of electoral gains.

The Janata Dal's version of secularism has been the promotion of both casteism and minority communalism. In 1943 Jinnah propounded the strategy of combining backward Hindus and Muslims, suggesting to Fazlul Haque to try the experiment in Bengal. Fazlul Haque did not follow his advice, the two-nation theory being so stridently propounded by Jinnah at that time left little scope for him to adopt this course of action himself. The Janata Dal has now been trying to implement Jinnah's strategy. Its leading lights have been paying obeisance to the Shahi Imam whom the party appears to have adopted as its patron saint. It has been obtaining *Fatwas* from him during elections. A leader who talks of Muslim Indian rather than Indian Muslim and who has been an activist of Babri Masjid Committee, has a pride of place in the party. Not satisfied with only a parallel personal law code, he is party to the idea of having a parallel judicial system. Islamic courts are to be set up all over the country to try cases arising of family disputes in accordance with the Shariat and Muslims are to be advised to refrain from taking such cases to the normal courts of law.

The Communist parties may have opposed the Quit India movement in 1942, supported the demand for Pakistan in 1947, hailed Chairman Mao as their Chairman in 1962 and also supported the Black Emergency in 1975 but their secular record has been better than that of other political parties. This may be because in Communist philosophy, religion has been decried as the opium of the masses.

However, strangely the CPM Politbureau has recently decided to propagate the Vivekanand version of Hinduism.

The BJP's strident support for the construction of Ram temple at Ayodhya and the outrage of December 6, has greatly sharpened the communal divide. Taking advantage of the feeling of resentment among Hindus, it raised the slogan of 'Justice for All and Appeasement of None.' This has earned the label of a communal party for BJP and made it into a favourite whipping horse of other political parties. The fact that the BJP has quite a few Muslims and its leadership has been repeatedly asserting that they do not want India to become a Hindu version of Pakistan, is being ignored.

The above analysis shows that we do not really have any secular political party in India. The difference between BJP and non-BJP parties is not of communalism and secularism but of electoral strategy. Whereas the non-BJP parties appear to be working overtime to woo the Muslim vote bank, BJP appears to have decided to go ahead without doing so and consolidating its support base among the Hindus.

Threats to Secularism

Having surveyed the steady erosion of secularism in the post-Nehruvian era we may now examine the current threats to secularism in the country. Basically the threats arise from three sources, namely, the Ayodhya dispute, the Kashmir problem and Hindu communalism. We need to go into the genesis of each of these.

Ayodhya Dispute

What the two nation theory had been in 1947, in terms of delivering a body-blow to secularism, the Ayodhya dispute is today. It has caused a similar if not a worse chasm as at the time of partition. The *Kar Sevaks* who went berserk on 6 December 1992 and demolished the Babri Masjid did an incalculable damage to Indian secular traditions and to the Hindu way of life. However, this dispute has a history of over four centuries. The Hindus maintain that the mosque built on the orders of Babar in 1528 was at the precise site where Lord Ram was born. A large Ram temple had existed at that site which was razed to the ground and Babri Masjid built. The Muslims do not accept that any temple was destroyed at that site to construct Babri Masjid. They have also questioned the authenticity of the site being the birthplace of Lord Ram. Some people have even gone to the extent of questioning whether Ram was a historical figure and whether he was born at Ayodhya at all. No doubt it is very difficult to reconcile these opposing views. However, an attempt should be made to view them in the right perspective. There may be no direct and convincing evidence of the destruction of any Hindu temple at that site in Ayodhya but the fact remains that during the mediaeval era thousands of Hindu temples were razed to the ground. Ayodhya being one of the holiest places for the Hindus, it is reasonable to presume that a large Ram temple may have existed there. The only explanation that no large and ancient Ram temple is to be found in Ayodhya today is the likelihood that it was demolished in an era when the destruction of Hindu temples was a common feature. Yet all this does not establish that a Ram temple existed at that site which was destroyed to build Babri Masjid. Religion is a matter of faith for which it is not necessary to adduce legal or historical evidence. Just as no proof is required to establish that Jesus was the son of Virgin Mary or the Prophet, who was illiterate, wrote the *Koran* as revealed to him by Allah, there is no evidence required to establish that Ram was a historical figure and was born at Ayodhya. However, the Hindu assertion that he was born at a precise site and not say ten to fifteen feet away appears unreasonable and cannot be supported on the basis of accepted Hindu belief. Be that as it may, sometime down the centuries, possibly in the time of Akbar, a very sensible compromise was evolved whereby a platform called Ram *Chabutra* was constructed within the precincts of Babri Masjid, where Hindus were permitted to offer prayers. However, Hindu-Muslim clashes are reported to have taken place and there is a mention of this in the documents of Nawab Wajid Ali Shah. An Italian traveller to Ayodhya in the seventeenth century wrote about the resentment among the Hindus at being deprived of the site where Lord Ram was born. All this was well before the arrival of the British in Ayodhya and the attempt to blame them for the dispute, as part of their divide and rule policy, appears far-fetched. The Maulvi of Fyzabad, one of the leaders of the 1857 struggle, had worked out an amicable solution to this controversy which had satisfied both the communities at that time.

This amity was short-lived and the controversy got revived with reports of occasional clashes on this issue. The last communal riot in Ayodhya during British rule took place in 1936 when Hindus damaged the Babri Masjid. A collective fine was imposed on the Hindus and the structure repaired. Against this long background of controversy, some Hindus on the night of 22nd December 1949 surreptitiously installed the idol of Ramlalla inside the mosque saying that it had itself come out from the bowels of the earth. The Government could have had the idol removed the next day or could have persuaded the local Muslim community to hand over the site to the Hindus as a gesture of goodwill. Unfortunately, the Government did not adopt either of these two courses. The doors of the mosque were locked and the case referred to law courts. For the last forty years and more this case remained lost in legal wrangles. However, the Hindus continued to offer prayers at the site from outside. The Muslims ceased to offer *Namaz* in or near the mosque. In 1987 the District Court ordered the opening of the locks at the mosque and Hindus were permitted to offer prayers inside the building, pending the legal cases regarding the Babri Masjid being finalised. It was at this stage that the rest of the country really got to know about this dispute as the political parties got into the fray along with religious leaders from both sides.

The Hindu leadership has failed to appreciate that their demand for undoing the past wrongs of history could only open a Pandora's box. Instead of exploiting religious sentiments on this highly emotive issue, they should have settled for constructing the Ram temple based on the Ram *Chabutra* and allowed the disused mosque to continue as a historical monument. The lack of vision of Hindu leadership was matched with an equal myopia of the Muslim leadership. They failed to appreciate the depth of Hindu sentiments which they could easily have done if only they could visualise a similar scenario at Mecca. A little generosity on the part of the Muslims could have radically changed the situation ushering a golden era of communal amity. After all, there was no special religious or architectural sanctity attached to the Babri Masjid like the mosque at Ajmer Shareef or the Jama Masjid at Delhi. There have been several instances of mosques having been demolished as in Saudi Arabia for construction of a palace or in Pakistan when the huge Mangla Dam water reservoir got constructed. Similarly, Hindu temples have been getting submerged in India when dams have been constructed or for that matter in Ayodhya itself when Hindus demolished the small temples near the disputed site to make room for the construction of the proposed Ram temple. Instead of showing a spirit of accommodation the attitude of both sides hardened. The Hindus started feeling that if their long-cherished desire of centuries did not get fulfilled now in Independent India, where they constituted the majority, they will be doomed to remain as underdogs for ever. The feeling on the Muslim side was that they could not afford to do a Munich at Ayodhya because that will only embolden the Hindus to make more such demands, particularly when there is already a simmering dispute of a similar nature at Mathura and Kashi. Political leaders and fundamentalists of both communities started exploiting this controversy for their own vested interests. In this process, Babri Masjid became the symbol of humiliation for the Hindus reminding them of their repeated defeats at the hands of the Muslim invaders and the systematic destruction of thousands of their temples. For the Muslims, Babri Masjid became a symbol of honour. It had to be preserved at all costs. The rigid and uncompromising attitude of the two sides was matched with the ineptness of the Government in dealing with the problem and ensuring the protection of Babri Masjid. Like a Greek tragedy events inexorably moved to the outrage that took place on December 6. Whatever may have been the merits of the case, the manner in which the structure was demolished by the frenzied mob was totally indefensible. The fact that a functioning 300-year-old Hindu temple was demolished at Ramna in Dacca in 1971 which has not been rebuilt to this day or some temples were demolished in Kashmir, cannot provide any justification for this senseless act which is so contrary to Hindu traditions. The plea that the Babri Masjid was a non-functional mosque does not in any manner mitigate matters. This single act of madness has caused an unprecedented chasm between the two communities. Hundreds of people got killed not only in India but also in Pakistan and Bangladesh in the wake of this incident. In Pakistan, Ministers with Government bulldozers led angry mobs in the destruction of Hindu temples. Government of India showed pusillanimity both during the events leading to December 6 and after. Nearly a year has elapsed and it has not come out with any concrete measures to tackle the problem beyond giving expression to platitudes. The situation appears reminiscent of 1949 when the Government had failed to take some positive measures which could have nipped the controversy in the bud. Some leading Hindu and Muslim citizens of Patna proposed to the Prime Minister that immediate televised excavation of the site be carried out in the presence of the representatives of the two communities. Depending upon the results of the excavation, the site be handed over to either the Muslims or the Hindus immediately. If excavation revealed that there had been no Hindu temple at that site then the Babri Masjid as it existed should be reconstructed. The Hindus could be allowed to construct the proposed Ram temple at Ram *Chabutra* or a little distance away. On the other hand if it got established that there was a temple at that site then the Hindus be allowed to construct a temple at that spot and the Babri Masjid reconstructed some distance away. The Muslim point of view before the demolition had been that if it could be convincingly proved that a temple existed at that site, they would give up their claim to it. This would be in accordance with Koranic injunction which forbids construction of mosque at the site where a place of worship of another faith may have existed. The merit of the proposal put up by some of the citizens of Patna was to provide an immediate solution to a highly controversial and long-standing dispute in a fair manner. Failure to act on this proposal or any other such proposal has only allowed the malignancy to continue festering with disastrous results. Maulana Waheedudin has put forward an eminently sensible solution. He has urged the Muslims to give up their claim at Ayodhya and to Hindus to do the same at Mathura and Kashi. This proposal has received a fair amount of support from both liberal Hindus and liberal Muslims. However, the present position appears to be of fundamentalists trying to call the shots from both sides wanting their place of worship constructed/reconstructed at that precise spot. The Muslim Personal Law Board and the Janata Dal politician Syed Shahabuddin have declared their intention to organise demonstrations in the streets from December 3 to 6 culminating in a mammoth rally at Delhi to press for their demand to reconstruct the mosque at that precise site. The nation is poised on a tinder box and such misconceived demonstrations can only lead to further disaster.

Kashmir Problem

The secessionist movement in Kashmir is another grave threat to secularism in India. In 1947 when the rest of the country reeled under the savage onslaught of communalism, Kashmir had been a shining example of secularism where communal amity prevailed. The legal accession of Kashmir to India was fully supported by Kashmir's undisputed popular leader, Sher-e-Kashmir. This accession got sanctified through a popular verdict given in the elections to Kashmir's Constituent Assembly and its proceedings. The 1965 war provided a convincing proof of the loyalty of the Kashmiri people to the Indian Union. They rendered invaluable help to the Security Forces in hounding out the 15,000 infiltrators sent to the State to foment a rebellion. Pakistan made three unsuccessful attempts to grab Kashmir trying out different techniques each time. In 1947 tribal raiders were sent in the hope that they would capture the State for Pakistan. In 1965 an attempt was made to foment a rebellion of the people of State through infiltrating 15,000 armed soldiers and saboteurs. In 1971 a conventional war with major offensive thrusts at Punch and Chhamb was tried out. Having failed in all these attempts Pakistan is currently engaged in a proxy war against India with the help of terrorists, armed, trained, financed and organised by its Inter-Services Intelligence (ISI) which is virtually a State within a State. This phase has coincided with the rearing up of a new generation in Kashmir after 1971 imbued with religious fanaticism and infiltrating the State administration in a planned and systematic manner. The culpable and inexcusable failure of the Central Government and the State Government in suitably dealing with this threat in the seventies and the eighties has compounded matters. The alienation of the people of Kashmir from India is now total and many have taken to terrorist violence aided by Pakistan with the aim of ensuring Kashmir's secession from India. Ethnic cleansing of the Kashmir Valley has been carried out with 300,000 Kashmiri Hindus forced to quit their homes and seek shelter in refugee camps at Jammu and Delhi. The Government has accepted this situation in a supine manner and our so-called secularist intelligentsia and political parties have maintained a total silence over this serious human issue, possibly because they fear that their raising this issue runs the risk of their being dubbed communal. If the 5 million Muslims in Kashmir manage to secede from India merely on account of their religion and provide yet another triumph for the pernicious two-nation theory, it will have a disastrous effect on secularism in India and on the 100 million Muslims of this country.

Hindu Communalism

As stated earlier, communalism is the antithesis of secularism. This applies equally to majority and minority communalism. However, on account of the logic of numbers, majority communalism is more dangerous than minority communalism. The Hindus constitute nearly 85% of the population of India and it must be accepted that India became a secular State primarily because the Hindus opted for secularism. It is commendable that they chose to do so at a time when Muslim communalism had extracted a heavy price in terms of the partition of the country. Yet the situation now has so developed that Hindu communalism has been more strident than ever before in our long history. The Sangh Pariwar has been in the van of Hindu communalism. It needs to be condemned for promoting what is being wrongly called the Hindutva wave. Hindutva should stand for Hinduism or Hindu values. These are most liberal and sublime. To brand Hindu obscurantism, fanaticism or fundamentalism as Hindutva is both wrong and mischievous. Without going into verbal semantics or apportioning blame for the present situation, we need to go into the factors that have contributed to the growth of Hindu communalism. Once these are clearly identified, efforts can be made to contain or neutralise them. This will be far more effective in curbing Hindu communalism than more condemnation of the Sangh Pariwar or of Hindu fundamentalism mistakenly called Hindutva, by the secularists.

The economic clout provided by petro dollars has fuelled Islamic fundamentalism the world over. Its effects are noticeable also in India. The Iranian Revolution was a triumph for Islamic obscurantism. With the collapse of the Soviet Union, the five Central Asian Muslim States have become vulnerable to the Islamic fundamentalist wave. Theocratic States like Saudi Arabia and Iran have been pouring billions of dollars in these countries, to promote Islamic fundamentalism. Liberal Muslim States like Egypt and Turkey are facing threats from Islamic militants within their countries. Nearer home, Afghanistan from being a secular Communist State has become a Revolutionary Islamic State. Bangladesh has discarded secularism and has become an Islamic Republic. The fanaticism now prevalent in that country is best illustrated by a recent incident. Ms. Tasleema Nasreen has written a book titled *Lajja*, depicting the harrowing tale of a Hindu family in Bangladesh after the demolition of the Babri Masjid. This has roused the ire of the *Mullahs*. Maulana Habibur Rahman, the head of Jamait-i-Islami in that country, has announced a reward of 50,000 takas to anyone who kills her. The Government of Bangladesh has withdrawn her passport and has declined to provide her security. The illegal infiltration of millions of Bangladesh refugees in the North-East is indicative of a sinister design. The so-called secular parties and the Government have turned a Nelson's eye to this grave problem for vote bank considerations. As for Pakistan, the treatment meted out to minorities in that country verges on being uncivilised. As a mark of their inferior status they have to carry a different coloured identity card and they are denied any position of authority in the administration. A separate electorate, unrelated to a constituency based on any geographical area, has been provided for them, to elect 10 members in the National Assembly of 217. They cannot directly vote in the election for a candidate who may become the Prime Minister or a party which may capture power. Besides growing international Islamic fundamentalism, there is also increased Muslim fundamentalism within India as shown in the recent bomb blasts in Bombay with help and guidance from Pakistan. Pakistan's victory over India in sports is often celebrated in Muslim localities in India with distribution of sweets. The ramifications of such insensitivity to nationalist sentiments need no elaboration. Asghar Ali Engineer, a leading Muslim liberal, has suggested a three-point strategy for combating communalism, namely, a sub-continental approach to the problem, gender justice for women and religious tolerance. Given the present scenario it appears utopian to hope that any sub-continental consensus can be developed on communalism. However, this issue is well worth being taken up in SARC. As for anti-national incidents within the country, these should be dealt with through the normal political and legal process.

The unfortunate developments in Ayodhya and Kashmir have had a disastrous impact on secularism. These issues have already been discussed at length. The former is a highly emotive matter and the latter with the ethnic cleansing of the Valley making 300,000 Kashmiri Hindus refugees in their own country, has become a very sensitive issue. An amicable solution of the Kashmir problem and winning the hearts and minds of the Kashmiri Muslims, are imperative for the survival of secularism in India. Muslims from the rest of the country should play a positive and active role in winning over Kashmiri Muslims.

The resentment among the Hindus on account of the State and the so-called secular parties trying to pamper Muslims through various gimmicks, is another important contributory factor towards the growth of Hindu communalism. As a case in point, a major change in the law of inheritance for Hindus was made giving daughters an equal share in their father's property when previously they used to have no share at all. Legislation on this was pushed through despite the opposition of orthodox Hindus and the then President of India, Dr. Rajendra Prasad, having reservations. On the other hand, in the case of Shah Bano, the Government caved in to the protests from orthodox Muslims and subverted the verdict of the apex court. Mention has already been made of State *Iftar* party to pander to Muslim sentiments and of no such State parties for other religious communities, as also of having compulsory national holiday for the Prophet's birthday when the birthdays of Lords Ram, Krishna and Shiva are optional national holidays. The privileges and facilities accorded to minority religious and educational institutions are not available for similar institutions of the Hindus. This led to the Ramakrishna Mission and the Arya Samaj declaring themselves to be non-Hindu organisations. The state must not only treat all its citizens alike but must be seen to be doing so.

Yet another contributory factor to the growth of Hindu communalism has been the double standards, verging on intellectual dishonesty, shown by some secularists. They take great care to respect Muslim sentiments and turn a blind eye to Muslim communalism, while they ride rough shod over Hindu sentiments and come down heavily on Hindu communalism. One must be even handed in the condemnation of communalism, no matter whether it is of the majority or the minority. The mute reaction of these secularists to the pillorying of a Muslim liberal in Patna for giving a perfectly sensible interpretation of *Kafir*, to the agitation against another liberal

Muslim, the Pro Vice-Chancellor of Jamia Millia, for his views on the ban imposed on Salman Rushdie's book or now the Muslim Personal Law Board's declaration to organise Islamic Courts, stands out in sharp contrast to their denunciation of Hindu protests against the objectionable poster in the recent *Sahmat* exhibition, showing Sita as the sister of Ram. Some secularists have been asserting that this panel did not hurt Hindu sentiments and the fascist forces led by the *Sangh Pariwar* had raised an unnecessary objection. Obviously, these secularists are living in an ivory tower and are totally ignorant of ground realities. From the time of *Rig Veda*, incestuous marriage is not permitted among the Hindus. Unlike other communities, where marriage between first cousins is not only permitted but encouraged, Hindus try to trace ancestry of a couple back to seven generations and if there is any blood relationship between them, they are not permitted to marry. Against this background to depict that Ram, who is universally worshipped by Hindus as Maryada Purshottam, married his own sister, cannot but grievously hurt Hindu sentiments. The attempt to defend the dubious historicity of the Buddhist Dasrath Jataka where this has been stated, is unfortunate. It can only be viewed as calculated blasphemy by the common Hindu. Some secularists have also chosen to defend this highly objectionable panel from another angle. Their plea is that the right to information is a fundamental right and the people should not be prevented from knowing the Dasrath Jataka version. Those interested in research can certainly study the Dasrath Jataka which is not banned but showing a highly objectionable panel whose historical veracity is highly doubtful in an exhibition is a totally different matter. The right to information has to be occasionally curtailed in the larger interests of the society. During communal riots, the right to information about the numbers killed by communities is rightly curtailed. Similarly, despite this right, restrictions are rightly placed on pornography. The right to information cannot be allowed to ride rough shod over the religious sentiments of a community. It would be very wrong to display excerpts from Salman Rushdie's book or from Outline of World History by H.G. Wells containing derogatory references to the Prophet. It would also be equally wrong to organise an exhibition and show extracts from the work of a recent research scholar who claims to have deciphered the Dead Sea scrolls and has come to the conclusion that Jesus Christ did not die on the Cross. He lived for many years after the Crucifixion and during that period , he got married and had children. The double standards shown by some intellectuals claiming to be secular tend to suggest that to them secularism means being anti-Hindu.

Conclusion

In 1947 when communalism had registered a triumph over secularism leading to the partition of the country, we had a galaxy of truly eminent leaders, the like of whom are not born in every generation. We had amongst us great leaders like Gandhi, Nehru, Patel, Azad and so on. The extent of communalisation of Hindus was also not so great. Thus we could successfully nurture secularism in the Nehruvian era. A very rapid decline in all spheres commenced in the post-Nehruvian period. We have seen the repeated body-blows being dealt to secularism in recent times. The sharp rise of Hindu communalism or Hindu backlash is closely connected with the rise of international Islamic fundamentalism. We have now no Gandhi, Nehru, Patel or Azad with us. The quality of our present political leaders is so pathetically poor. In the circumstances, the future of secularism in our country would appear to be very bleak. Yet secularism is a pearl of great value which we can ill-afford to lose. It must be nourished and preserved at all costs, in keeping with our rich and unique traditions. This is also an inescapable imperative for a pluralistic society like ours. We must suitably deal with the threats to secularism, arising from the Ayodhya dispute, the Kashmir problem and the alarming rise of Hindu communalism. The Ayodhya dispute must be resolved amicably in a realistic manner with both communities showing wisdom and vision. Kashmir cannot be allowed to secede under any circumstance and the present alienation of the Kashmiri Muslims has to be removed by winning the battle for their hearts and minds. The factors contributing to the growth of Hindu communalism must be contained and neutralised. These are more dangerous for our secular ideals than any activities of the *Sangh Pariwar*. In the long term, the spread of education and the inclusion of the essentials of the glorious aspects of all religions in school textbooks will go a long way towards removing misconceptions and promoting amity. Religious harmony and tolerance are the bedrocks of secularism.

3

SECULARISM—PRECEPT AND PRACTICE

Bindeshwar Pathak

The power of politicians to twist the meanings of words has always intrigued me. They have been doing it all these years just to suit their political objectives; not in any case to solve problems or create an acceptable social order. One case in point is the word "secularism". By no stretch of imagination, this word suggests a religion-neutral social order, or a situation in which an "un-Godly" political dispensation will take over like those by Marxists.

But over the years, secularism has come to indicate a situation opposite of theoratic state or religion-based social or political setup. No wonder, there has been a continuing debate on the interpretation of the word "secularism". Religious extremists have also been proclaiming themselves as secular. Hindus say *Ram Rajya* is a secular social order while Muslims say *Shariat* laws on personal conduct are about the best thing to happen to mankind. It is difficult to deny or confirm any of these interpretations. They may be right; they may be wrong, I don't know.

But what has come to be known as a secular social order is truly not a religion-neutral system. Nor can it be equal respect to all setup (*Sarva Dharma Sambhava*). It is quite natural for a Hindu to respect his religion more than others. This is true of the practitioners of other religions also. Therefore, to say that state leaders will have equal respect to all is false.

Secularism as a concept has a beginning in the medieval times when there was a continuing conflict between the Church and the State. The Pope used to make and unmake the Kings and the Queens in Europe. So much so, that sovereign states had to pay tributes to the Vatican to ensure that they are not dethroned by the Pope who considered himself as the rightful heir to the throne of God. And, hence, ordained to look after the Christian world.

There was a revolt against this social order and, finally, the Church was separated from the State. But in India, there was no such system. Religion has always been a private concern and the priests never interfered with the functioning of the state though the royal priests had considerable influence over Kings. There was no equivalent to the Vatican in India. But, with the rise of fundamentalism, there has been the mixing of religion with politics. And now politics is saturated with false religious concept. And the state, which is supposed to be religion-neutral, has taken up the role of the church also.

While the civil law in India recognizes the personal laws of different communities, criminal law has always been uniformly applicable to all. The amendment of the Code of Criminal Procedure, therefore, convinced many Hindus that the Government would bend to please reactionary Muslims. In a way, the irrational behaviour of VHP in Ayodhya was closely linked to the irrational reaction of a group of Muslims to the Shah Bano case. I am on record in the past and I reiterate here that while every community has the right to follow its customary rules, redressal by the courts should be available only under uniform civil laws.

For that matter we have failed to give effect to the provisions of Article 44 of the Constitution. We have deviated from the secular status of the Republic. The fear of radical Muslims that common civil code will dilute Islam is baseless because even Sections 125, 126 and 127 of the unamended CrPC state that a magistrate will take due cognizance of any payment made to a divorced woman under customary or personal law. Even a uniform civil code, therefore, can take into account customary law, but with the proviso that the procedures will be uniform.

The question of religion assumed significance in India at the end of the 19th century as a consequence of the demand of the nationalist leaders for representative government. With it began the modern political process. Religion supplied vocabulary for nationalism in West Asia, Northern Ireland and South Asia. Even if the origin of the conflict is economic, it developed religious connotations over a time.

In such a situation, we should work to move the entire political process from religious ties to a firmer constitutional and religion-neutral basis. However, though we opted for a liberal democratic order, the general nature of Indian polity has been far from secular. Democracy evolved in certain Western countries with specific characteristics, with Great Britain being the ideal type and the USA and France being the variants of this liberal democratic model.

When we adopted the Westminster model, we created the form of this edifice but the substance and context of it was absent. For instance, the three most essential ingredients of a true democratic order are: access to resources, access to speedy justice and access to education. All these have eluded most people in India, the consequences of which are there for all to see. We are not able to work out a political arrangement and an economic order which can create a viable society. In a situation where the basics are denied, the commitment to principles like secularism looks hollow, especially when politicians are playing foul in the game. Religion, caste and economic disparities have made Indian society most combustible in the world.

The vitality of a political system is largely sustained by the faith that the ordinary people will have social and economic justice. In our inability to achieve these, we reflect an alienated culture rather than a participatory one. By now it is well-established that religious fundamentalism takes root only under a political order which is not trusted by most people.

The healing process has to begin with an admission of past mistakes by all the political parties and groups which have used religion and caste to further their advantages electorally. In the process, they have ignored the important fact that both religion and caste-based politics are pre-modern and antithetical to the individualistic and libertarian assumptions of liberal democracy.

Since all the political groups flaunt variants of this pre-modern attitude, they have to distance themselves from the past. This will also reduce the patron-client relationship within the political framework which has helped perpetuate the oligarchic nature of our political parties. The State funding of elections is a necessity but it has to be linked to the democratization of the political parties with the U.S. primary system being a model to match. This is to be followed by the enforcement of the rule of law, creating credible institutions and enhancing the prestige of the judiciary by expeditious and affordable judicial process. The executive action must look well-thought out and impartial. Once a right decision has been taken by the judiciary, it must not be turned down by an executive action or by securing a parliamentary majority as happened in the case of Shah Bano.

Coupled with this new political action, we also have to accept the fact that both important religious creeds practised in India, like any religion anywhere, contain within themselves large groups of pre-modern orthodox elements which have to be reformed to bring them at par with the dominant practices of the modern world.

Tagore explains it succinctly by pointing out that the advent of the West through British rule with its implications was much more far-reaching in its impact than the entire basis, period. Historically the change was from the Islamic to British rule, but in reality it was a change from the medieval to the modern era. For Tagore, the first major attack on Indian society came from Islam. But it was a religious creed that also belonged to the old East and, like Hindus, it was pre-modern. As a consequence, it was also confined to the past.

The expansion and consolidation of the empire was brought about by force but it did not have any novelty. And, once Islam had settled down in India on a permanent basis, a conflict took place between two traditional orders, between one faith and another. The important fact to note is that though Islam came from outside and settled in India, it did not lead to a widening of horizon.

In other words, in the life of an average Indian Islam did not bring any significant change. Our vision was limited to the village life. Full of rituals and traditional customs. Till the advent of the British, medieval administration and society had no conception of justice. This was reflected in the equation of the King with God. This medievalism stunted the growth of society and, as Tagore described it, lulled India into a death-like sleep. It is in this context that the role of Rammohan Roy becomes historic: for, he was the first to envisage a modern, rational society based on reason and rule of law.

What is striking in our earlier assessments is that this criticism of medievalism was not confined to Islamic rule. It is equally critical of outmoded Hindu practices. Even the Marathas were castigated by Jadunath Sarkar for not initiating or incorporating new ideas which was one of the major reasons for their downfall.

It is equally important to remember the saying of Bankim Chandra Chatterjee that the religious differences between the Hindus and Muslims were not an issue comparable to the issues of poverty and development. An independent nation may become dependent for all practical purposes if it does not grow out of poverty. In this context, Chatterjee cites the example of England under the Normans and India under Aurangzeb. In contrast to Aurangzeb'a India, Akbar's India was free. For Chatterjee, the criteria of a nation's status are not race and religion but development and growth.

India displays great ethnic and cultural diversity. Viewing it against the homogeneous Western States, one may wonder how far this diversity is consistent with national unity. But this is what India has always been in the past. The Indian idea of unity is not uniformity but harmony.

Indian society was born in sylvan surroundings. The cradle of Indian civilization was the *vana,* forest. In this tropical scene as against the sand or snow, there was luxuriant growth all round. And so in the Indian consciousness, diversity is "natural", it is good and right. Even our religious beliefs are offshoots of this situation. If there can be an infinite variety of flora and fauna in a forest, why not a multiplicity of gods and goddesses as expressors of divinity? This acceptance of diversity as the "norm" was also reflected in Indian social oganizations. Tribes were not steamrolled into a few homogeneous classes; they were allowed to maintain their separate identity as a caste or subcaste in a well-integrated Indian society.

There was no imposition of any one model and no dominance of any one race, tribe or geographical area, but a massive crossfertilization of ideas and institutions. Hinduism with its Sanskritic base was a Sangha confederate of innumerable religious beliefs and life-styles. In this flowering of what Toynbee described as the "Indo

Civilization", Siva and Kali were clearly pre-Vedic and the dark-skinned Rama and Krishna were not textbooks Aryans. Without its sheer resilience, Hindu society probably would never have survived the Muslim vandalism.

And we do not need to exaggerate the seriousness of dissidence. Dissent is inherent in a democracy. Even small countries like England, Belgium and Spain have serious separatist ethnic movements on their lands. In contrast the separatist demands based on religion in India are confined to a few areas. As of secularism, the concept becomes relevant in a multi-religion society. It should be remembered that unlike Christianity, — and Islam, Hinduism provides for dissent: "Ekam sad, vipra bahuda vadanti".

But it is this fear that causes the Muslims to make issues out of *Shariat* Law. They use it as a barricade to protect their separate identity. The traditional Hindu will never object to their separate identity. But the fear remains. And so the "Muslim Problem" remains. There is a Muslim problem in several countries; and problems of centuries do not lend themselves to instant solutions. And, with that is attached the question of secularism. This quarrel over secularism is largely political and once the state clearly indicates that it is firm on rule of law, this problem will vanish.

To think of India as a dominant Hindu majority, bossing over minorities, is wholly unrealistic. Who is the majority in India? In religious-cultural terms, we certainly have a Hindu majority. But considering the fact that Hinduism is not so much a religion as a way of life, and Hindus do not act as one except when attacked, for that matter, secularism as a concept is irrelevant.

The reasons for the general unhappiness have nothing to do with our cultural and ethnic diversity; they have everything to do with the general mismanagement of our polity, our economy and our national laws.

Hence, I consider that secularism is a flawed concept, made more unnecessary because this was already there in India's multi-cultural and multi-religious society. Yes, politicians have made it an issue and a very serious one at that. But politicians should not forget that if religion is allowed to dominate politics, priests will rule the country. This is not an acceptable situation to me.

4

SECULARISM IN INDIA : THE KEY ISSUES

Ali Ashraf

Certain concepts run the risk of being turned into popular cliches. Secularism is one such concept. The unfortunate history of communal politics in India makes it generally difficult to achieve emancipation from contemporary political distortions as well as historical antecedents of this sub-continent. One obvious result is that secularism is conceived mostly in the context of Hindu-Muslim conflict. Not that this context is irrelevant. On the contrary it is an important and crucial dimension of some of the major political developments of this sub-continent. It is, however, necessary to bear in mind that this is not the only dimension of secularism, and its other aspects are equally vital. The concept of secularism, therefore, needs to be analyzed in its totality—as it affects the total social, economic and political life of our country. Once this is clear, the Hindu-Muslim context can be put in correct perspective. The task, therefore, is to analyze the socio-economic context, and not merely the one issue of communal problem.

I

The question of secularism is undoubtedly bound up with the issue of communal politics which has centered around the political relationship between the two major communities of India. The separatist politics of Indian Muslims before Independence beginning with the establishment of the Muslim League and culminating in the partition of the country had historical origins and need not be discussed here. One can identify two aspects of this problem—the exploitation of communalism by the British Government and the readiness with which both the Hindus and the Muslims fell a victim to the politics of communalism. The first was of course the usual 'divide and rule' policy of an imperial power. The second seems to have emanated from the sense of insecurity of both the communities. The Muslim fears of being swamped by the 'brute' majority of the Hindus lay at the root of a misconceived two-nation theory. The Hindu leadership also showed a lack of self-confidence and began to 'react' to Muslim communalism in a defensive manner. The emergence of Bangladesh, 25 years after the partition of India, has taught us a lesson that a political system to be viable and durable, not to talk of being legitimate, must ensure justice, freedom and dignity of all its people. Religion like language may help to bring a people together, but cannot be used to legitimize tyranny and oppression. The concern for justice, freedom and dignity is now too strong to be compromised by a false allegiance to 'religion' which may be invoked to trample upon these basic values.

As against the fate of Pakistan, the successful way in which free India has managed to survive as one polity amidst the diversities of language and religion is in a large measure due to her successful experiment in a democratic system based on reconciliation and accommodation of various religious and ethnic groups. India's attempt to achieve national unity amidst regional and parochial forces is due to its pluralistic and participatory democracy. And in this respect the unique cultural tradition of tolerating diversities and allowing various religious and ethnic groups to carve out an autonomous existence within a common cultural framework makes it possible and almost natural for India to do the same in the political sphere. The tradition of co-existence and tolerance of different religious sects paves the way for a similar exercise in political pluralism. Hence secularism in the sense of political neutrality towards religions is the hallmark of India's traditional and contemporary history. The right to religious freedom guaranteed by the Indian Constitution and avoidance of discrimination on religious grounds is in tune with this aspect of India's tradition. Secularism in this sense cannot be called the gift of westernization but reflects the catholic spirit of respect for different paths towards spirituality that has characterized most of the phases of India's indigenous tradition.

The question of separation between the church and the state is, therefore, not a issue in India. The distinction has always been made between the political and socio-cultural domains and each was allowed to function autonomously within its own spheres of activities. Hence, the neutrality of the state vis-a-vis various religions and their equal treatment at the hands of the state. In modern times, Gandhi exemplified this tradition, and he not only disputed the religious bases of nationalism but also accorded equal respect to all religions. His prayers including verses from many religious scriptures and his constant emphasis on the essential and fundamental unity of all religions highlighted the unique Indian approach to religious truth and also provided the cultural underpinning for secularism. Indeed seen from this perspective, even this disavowal of separation between religion and politics is quite consistent with secularism because religion in his sense was not to be identified with any particular religion or denomination but with the essential and common element of all religions, which cannot violate the moral integrity and dignity of all men. Secularism in his sense is not a denial of religion but an affirmation of its authentic moral and spiritual values.

The challenge to secularism in this sense, however, comes from fundamentalists of all religions who believe in the monopoly and finality of their own religious truths as literally interpreted from the religious texts and traditional dogmas. The political incarnation of such religious fundamentalism is to be found in both the Hindu and the Muslim communities. The Jamaat-e-Islami and the RSS reject the pluralist approach to religions and consider the state as the organ of a religious community. There is no place of equality for a minority religion. The political system is only seen as a superstructure of which the religious community is the substructure. From the point of view of politics, the real danger from such political movements lies in their totalitarianism, which is a threat not only to the secular but also to the democratic system of the country. Advocates of totalitarian ideology, whether Muslim or Hindu, pose identical challenge because, these anti-secular forces are also anti-democratic. The tolerance extended so far to such anti-democratic organizations is a tribute to Indian democracy. The question may, however, be asked whether India can and should allow such organizations to operate and subvert its democratic system.

II

Another aspect of secularism touches upon the role of the state in social change. In spite of the political neutrality towards religions,

Government of India has been responsible for quite a few important legislative reforms in the civil laws governing the majority community. This role of the government has been accepted by the Hindus despite some controversy over the merits of specific legislative provisions. Thus the Hindus have available to them an important agency of social change in the positive role of the government. This agency has been so far denied to the Muslims mainly due to the deliberate government policy of non-interference in the civil laws governing the minorities. This raises two questions from the standpoint of the state : non-interference means abdication of authority and may imply a constraint on the policy-making power of the government. Is it compatible with the sovereign power of a government? And even though the answer can be given that non-interference is the result of political policy rather than political incompetence, the next question arises whether or not the government should initiate reformist policies for all religious communities in keeping with the broad policies of the government or vital interests of the state. Put in an extreme form the question is this : in the event of a conflict between the national policy and the sectarian interest of a particular community, which is going to prevail? The inevitable secular answer is that the national policy and the vital interest of the state prevail over sectarian policies of a particular group or community. However both the question and the answer framed in this way are more academic than pragmatic. Without questioning the sovereignty of the state, the question can be reduced to a pragmatic issue : whether the government must impose a reform and provoke political consequences which may not be consistent with the larger interests of the state? In particular given the democratic polity in an open society, committed to the policy of social and political pluralism, it may appear to be more expedient to leave the question of social change and reform to the initiative of each particular community.

This may be a wise or expedient policy from the view-point of the government. Both the secularists and the Hindu extremists however severely attack this policy of the government. They consider the policy of non-intervention as appeasement of the Muslims whose exemption from the civil laws confers upon them a privilege. The question is whether from the standpoint of social reform the policy of non-intervention implies a privilege or neglect of minority communities. The orthodox Muslim may even consider the government intervention as an attack on his religion. Leaving aside both protagonists and opponents of intervention, and from the viewpoint of social change and reform if the government does not mean to intervene in the personal laws of Muslims, and if it is granted that there is need for some change in the personal laws of Muslims, the policy of non-intervention amounts to a denial of political means of reform and social change for a particular community. It seems that given the fact of government non-intervention and the lack of organized initiative for reform in the Muslim community, this community is reaping the consequences of 'benign neglect' of both the government and God. The Muslim community it seems has forfeited the right to guidance from both the secular and non-secular leadership of a modern type. This then is another challenge to secularism in India. One can only hope that in absence of government initiative, Muslim leadership would emerge to organize support for reform among the Muslims. The non-intervention of the government places greater responsibility upon the Muslims to consider and initiate processes of change in the personal laws of the community. Unfortunately the initiative of Muslim leadership has been tardy and the response of the community much worse.

III

The Renaissance and the Enlightenment were the two intellectual movements that may be described as the main sources of secularism. The Renaissance represents the cultural awakening after a long and deep slumber of the mediaeval times, dominated by feudal social structure and ecclesiastical authority of the Church. The revolt against the inhibitions and constraints imposed by the feudal society and the church and the urge for freedom in all spheres of life was a revolt against authority and irrationality. The Protestant ethics stressed the economic achievement in this world and Calvin's theory of predestination was interpreted in terms of economic success as a portent of blessedness in the Hereafter. The Enlightenment likewise rejected the authority of religion and tradition, emphasized the perfectability of man through reason and held out the prospect of infinite progress. It sought to achieve not morality but happiness here and now. The appropriate question for the Philosophy of the Enlightenment was not—Am I right? or Am I Just? but Am I happy? This concerns with happiness on this earth rather than with the Hereafter, the concern with this world and its mundane affairs was the essence of Enlightenment that represented the spirit of secularism as it developed in the West. Marx who rejected the Liberal and Laissez-faire doctrine underlying the political philosophy of Enlightenment has been described as the illegitimate child of this movement in that he shared the secular concerns of Enlightenment regarding human perfectability and progress on this earth and the rejection of religious concern with the other world. Indeed the empiricism of Locke and the Utilitarianism of Bentham and Mill—important stands in liberal political philosophy and the dissenting voice of levellers and socialists mingled to highlight the worldly concerns of material well-being. Utilitarianism rejected the metaphysical considerations and interpreted good in terms of whatever is conducive to happiness. In its concern with this world, the secular West upheld the ideals of reason and rationality. The development of science and technology, involving questions of proof, verification and workability, further streamlined the trend towards secularisation. The upshot of all this has been strong orientation towards materialistic and this-worldly achievement.

The conflict between the secular and the ecclesiastical, beginning with the Renaissance, has culminated in the modern conflict between the secular scientific materialism and traditional religious obscurantism. It is 'either or' dichotomy between secularism and obscurantism that simplifies and even distorts the current discussion about secularism in India. It has become this or that world. The Hindu belief in *Karma* and *Maya* and the Muslim concern with the 'paradise' are said to have led to a neglect of this world and its problems. The sight of illiterate, poor and sick people, lacking in the attitudes of skills necessary for a healthy living, and engrossed in discharging the 'religious' rituals is a constant reminder of the fact that something has gone wrong somewhere. In such cases it is hard to escape the conclusion that the health and dignity of human beings is being sacrificed at the altar of some misconceived 'superior' and supernatural norms. It is in this context that secularism is invoked to bring about a much needed reform in the perspective of all those who suffer from religious obscurantism. But one does not have to be an atheist or an agnostic to appreciate the value of a clean, healthy and happy life on this earth.

Unfortunately, in many parts of our country religious formalism and fundamentalism dominate the social life of a large number of Hindus and Muslims with the result that they do not attach importance to the interests of this work. The neglect of this world in most cases is almost a pathological phenomenon and probably an escape mechanism for personal failure or inability to solve mundane problems. It is not uncommon for both the Muslims and the Hindus to spend their life's savings, and in fact even to incur debts, over useless religious ceremonies. This utterly uneconomic and irrational attitude is in sharp contrast to the values of simplicity, economy, cleanliness, hard work and self-reliance.

It would be unnecessary to contrast such religious obscurantism as we witness in India with the "protestant ethic" of the West. In our own country one can see the contrast between the indolent and improvident life-style of a community or region and the clean, frugal and industrious life-style of another community or region. The parallel existence of various "traditions" is an important aspect of our national life. Some traditions appear quite modern, while others are traditional. The *Gujrati Bani* "ethic" for example represents the values of simplicity, cleanliness, hard work and entrepreneurship whereas the dominant ethos in the tradition of the Ganga-belt is characterized by feudal extravagance and inertia. It would be completely erroneous to interpret Indian secularism only in political terms and neglect questions of life-styles in terms of attitudes and capability to achieve basic economic conditions necessary for an honest and dignified life. This-worldly values do not imply cross-materialism, unlimited wants and vulgar display of wealth. The ideals of simple living, limited wants and austerity as preached and practised by Gandhi affirm rather than deny the essential secular concerns of his thought and action. There is a vital difference between the "voluntary poverty" of Gandhi and the miserable existence of millions of our countrymen. It is religious obscurantism, not genuine spirituality, that poses a challenge to secular rationality and posits a false dichotomy between this world and the other world resulting in the obsession with the other world to the neglect of this world. With most people in India the "sacred" still prevails over the secular, which properly understood is not only consistent with but indeed a condition for sound moral life. Spirituality does not deny this world, it only seeks to transcend it. True religion does not reject this world, it only puts the mundane in its proper place.

The above observations assume the need for reform and change. There are two kinds of extreme views on this. The traditional fundamentalist view believes in the laws of God. The argument is simple—how can human laws be superior to God's laws. The other extremist view emphasizes not so much reform as transformation. This view also adopts a simple stance that all tradition is bad and irrelevant and must be overthrown. Among the Hindus while the Jagat Guru Shankaracharya of Puri may be said to represent the orthodox approach to religion, M.M. Roy and his followers represent the other view of total rejection of the religion. However, there has developed in Hinduism a moderate stand of reconciliation between the secular and the religious. Both Vivekanand and Gandhi emphasized the value of the temporal as well as the eternal, and spirituality was interpreted in a way so as to emphasize the essentially humanist values implicit in religion. In modern India one can observe different economic subcultures ranging from the poor and decadent peasantry and the middle classes in the erstwhile zamindari areas of the eastern region to the enterprising and hardworking peasants and businessmen of the western and northern regions. The differences in regional and social subcultures reflected in different levels of economic achievement.

Among the Muslims, religious fundamentalism can be seen in their attitudes and life-styles, and above all in the philosophy of Jamaat-e-Islami. The "transformation" view on the other hand is represented by such ardent secularists as Hamid Dalvai and the Marxists. These views of course represent the basic conflict between secularism and fundamentalism. It is true that the *Quran* has recurrent references to the Hereafter, and to the reward of the Hereafter that is better than the enjoyment of this world. But the reference to the Hereafter appears essentially as an ethical standard of guidance for conduct in this world. As the *Quran* says :

> "Wealth and children are an ornament of life of the world. But the good deeds which endure are better in the Lord's sight for reward, and better in respect of hope."

The emphasis is thus on the good deeds and it would be travesty of the spirit of Islam, nay of any religion, to interpret the good deeds in the sense of performance of rituals divorced from the problems of life. The good deeds refer to deeds showing charity and concern for others. Religion in this sense is not opposed to secularism. Indeed it only seeks to provide a standard and a value by which to judge the secular life. The secular by itself is unable to provide a standard of judgement which must come from outside the egoistic pursuit of self-interest. The danger in a purely secular approach to life may be the absence of a moral standard to judge what is right and wrong. The philosophy of utilitarianism, for example, has been criticised on this ground that the principle of pleasure can degenerate into a hedonistic code of conduct and no community or society can endure on the egoistic principle of pleasure. Rousseau's criticism of the Enlightenment philosophy and its stress on happiness is well taken. His general will provides a standard of a general welfare by which to judge the actions of an individual or a community. Likewise the Hereafter is a standard of judgement and a source of inspiration for human activities without being completely lost in this world. Religion need not, therefore, be opposed to secularism and only seeks to inculcate a sense of detachment. It seeks to uphold a norm of duty or piety by which the secular must be evaluated. It is, therefore, wrong to say that the intention in a religion is to establish a dichotomy between this world and the Hereafter. Its intention must be interpreted to be the opposite, i.e., to affirm the great value of things secular by holding them to the mirror of the other world.[1]

Thus, Whitehead identifies God as "that factor in the universe whereby there is importance, value and ideal beyond the actual. It is clear that the complete identification of secularism with materialism and atheism and the rejection of religious values is neither necessary nor desirable. This is also out of tune with the tradition of genuine spirituality in which India takes legitimate pride. The proclamation of God's death in the West not only offends our religious susceptibility but would be subversive of the moral foundation of balanced and same worldly progress. The purpose of this rather long discussion was only to show that the dichotomy fixed between Religion and secularism is false. Gandhiji was right when he rejected this dichotomy. Religious fundamentalism introduces a serious distortion, and this is very ominous in certain religious movements such as Jamaat-e-Islami which seek to pit the laws of God against the laws of man in the wrong way. The laws of God like natural law can be interpreted only in terms of certain fundamental and universal moral values rather than detailed legislation about human affairs irrespective of the social and economic circumstances.

This can be seen in the diversities of tradition in Islamic countries. Pakistan and Bangladesh nearer home and for long part of the same country, display wide cultural differences despite a common faith. The basic norms of Islam do not ensure a common culture, and the cultural differences among various Muslim countries are as striking as among other countries of the world. Every religion has a hierarchy of values ranging from the basic beliefs to rituals and social and legal codes. The rituals and codes are contingent on social and cultural circumstances, and the basic religious norms must be left to the interpretation of man. The institutions of marriage, the status and role of woman or property rights, for example, cannot be final and must be adapted to serve the social and moral needs of man. The resistance to such adaptation and reforms on the ground of religious fundamentalism is a challenge not only to secularism but also to Religion, both of which must aim to bring about man's moral and material progress.

IV

A salient feature of the Indian society is a high degree of particularism. The ascriptive and particularistic roots of caste and community affiliation set the framework in which our society and polity function. The significance of particularism to secularism is that it limits the scope of social and political participation in the various spheres of national life. The traditional practice of purity and pollution, the various social and religious rituals and constraints on social interactions inhibit realistic and intimate knowledge and understanding of the members of one community by another. It is, therefore, not surprising that even much talked about social change has not been able to remove the barriers to inter-caste and inter-community integration. The village of course is the great preserver of traditional rigidities. The rural social structure perpetuates the caste, community and class segregation to an extent that even the introduction of modern political institutions has not significantly changed the pattern of communal participation in social and political process. But the persistence of such barriers is found even in urban areas, where segregation in settlement and social activities continues. This is true even in metropolitan and new industrial towns. Each community further entertains stereotypes and images of others which are seriously prejudicial to mutual understanding. It is common to find that a member of one community cannot get a house on rent in an area inhabited mostly by another community. Even the participation in each other's holidays and other social functions is rare. Given this kind of pervasive segregation it is difficult for various religious and ethnic communities to develop inter-community integration.

The barriers to communication and participation have disastrous consequences for the development of a secular culture. These barriers not only foster ignorance of each other but also perpetuate prejudices and social and political exclusiveness which, in an economy of poverty, breeds imaginary grievances and frustrations. In such a situation the slightest provocation leads to communal violence thus further adding to the exclusiveness and separation of communities. When people do not share life experience together, they do not develop common identity or at least mutual understanding and respect. Religion is one factor in sharing life together but hardly the only one. In fact language and neighbourhood may offer continuous opportunities for sharing life together. Many of us would not have failed to notice that those who speak the same language make better friends than even members of the same religion. Before the emergence of Bangladesh one could see abroad the close friendship between the Bengalis of Calcutta and Dacca or between Punjabis of Amritsar and Lahore. Speaking the same language, sharing the same songs and jokes and enjoying the same food foster social solidarity no less than sharing the same religious rites and rituals. The lack of social affinity between the East and West Pakistan before 1971 was enough to confirm that offering Id prayers together was neither a necessary nor a sufficient condition for national or social integration.

It is thus important to bear in mind that religious affinity and nationalism are not at all identical. Nationalism as a powerful secular force is based upon shared experience in the birth life of the polity. There is a natural love for land of one's birth, the friends and neighbours with whom one grows up and shares the day-to-day experiences, the local food and sports. These constitute vital stuff of which one's life is made of. Lack of love for these can be only pathological arising from a total alienation from one's self and surroundings. The trouble with a movement like Pan-Islamism has been precisely this — it ignores the secular forces of social solidarity. Life is not built upon 'ideas' alone, there must be some social base to make an idea a reality. The ideology of Pan-Islamism before independence must be treated as a psychopathological reflection of a schizophrenic community. The continuing reference of Mr. Bhutto to the 'Ideology of Pakistan' reflects a perverse disregard of trans-religious values and secular forces underlying social solidarity of a people.

The Hindu Mahasabha and Jan Sangh theory of an exclusive Hindu Rashtra or 'Indianization' reveals the reverse side of the same coin. Indian Muslims who share their life with their 'brothers' on this soil belong here and nowhere else in the world. The convergence of outlook between the Muslim and the Hindu communal elements is a challenge to Indian secularism and to national integration as well as to democracy. It is interesting to note that democracy as a system designed to provide maximum opportunities of participation in the social and political life is rejected by both Hindu and Muslim communal organizations.

The existence of separate Muslim political organizations such as the Muslim League (not to mention the Jamaat-e-Islami) is another threat to secular politics. It is argued by the champions of these separate political parties for Muslims that these parties are quite consistent with democracy because they ensure effective representation of the Muslims and in fact strengthen the democratic processes through active political participation. This argument is open to several objections. Communal parties fragment the party system and weaken the basis of democratic stability. To the extent the interests of a minority lie in the success of democracy, communal parties undermine their own long term interest. Most of the communal problems arise from social and economic backwardness and an effective way to serve the interests of Muslims is to participate more actively in the solution of common socio-economic problems. Communal parties divert the focus from such secular problems to essentially communal issues that are at best secondary in importance. And finally communal parties of one community are likely to strengthen and justify communal parties of other communities. Thus the existence of separate political parties for Muslims may secure a few legislative seats but is not conducive to the larger interests of the community as a whole.

These interests are primarily educational and economic. In addition to relying on the Government as citizens for the solution of their problems, there is nothing in the constitution of the political situation of the country to prevent the Muslims from establishing institutions of their own. Indeed that is hardly the problem. The Muslims suffer more from internal inhibitions than from external obstacles. The community has lost a sense of realism and a capacity for concrete socio-economic reform and finds in the alleged discrimination an alibi for its own lack of vision or competence. The undoubted difficulties that a sizeable minority community like the Muslims have to face in private or public employment is part of the larger problem of economic underdevelopment and social particularism. Hence the need of the hour is more and not less participation in the national effort to solve common secular problems.

Having said this, it would be only honest to mention that there is a tendency on the part of Indian scholars and intellectuals and policy-makers to disregard the dysfunctional consequences of particularism. It has been customary to emphasize the 'modern' functions of traditional social institutions like the caste. Caste as the most obvious factor in social particularism is said to perform the same functions as voluntary organizations in the West. For example they help the articulation and aggregation of interests, foster organized political participation and contribute to institutional participation and social mobility. These functions of the caste must be granted. However from a secular point of view, one should look upon not only the function but also the formation of the traditional institution. Their formation is ascriptive and not open to voluntary membership irrespective of caste, community or ethnic affiliation. The political process has a way of exploiting as well as correcting the dynamic of communal/ethnic political participation. But without social and cultural reorientation political mobilization is bound to remain basically sectarian, communal and particularistic. The abolition of discriminatory practices, of untouchability, of ethnic, regional and linguistic chauvinism is necessary condition for the development of an open and just society and humanist civic culture, without which genuine secularism will not grow.

REFERENCE

1. As Whitehead says :

   "God is that function in the world by reason of which our purposes are directed to ends which in our own consciousness are impartial as to our own interests. He is that element in life in virtue of which judgement stretches beyond *facts of existence to values of existence*. He is that element in virtue of which our purposes intend beyond values for ourselves to values for others. He is that element in virtue of which the attainment of such a value for others transforms itself into value for ourselves.

   "He is the binding element in the world. The consciousness which is individual in us, is universal in him. Love which is partial in us is all embracing in him. His purpose in the world is quality of attainment...

   "He is not the world, but the valuation of the world. In abstraction from the course of events, this valuation is a necessary metaphysical function."

5

ANATOMY OF COMMUNALISM

A.K. Lal

I

Communalism in the western industrial civilization refers to a state where the people in order to deal with the alienation and anonymity of deteriorating urban milieu favour revival of community institutions and values.[1] On occasions termed as fundamentalism it is seen as "a resolute retreat from the principles of modernity into the more comprehensible doctrine of tradition, a secure move into the past in the face of modernity's incomprehensibility and sufferings."[2] The term communalism has acquired a pejorative connotation in India as it implies a tendency on the part of a religious group to assert itself politically. It refers to a situation where relationship between communities is antagonistic. It leads to "a condition of suspicion, fear and hostility between members of different religious communities."[3] Communalism leads to sharpening of religious consciousness and is reflected in intensified passions. It finds expression in the riots. Such orientations and their manifestation are inclined to get embedded. It is an ideology "which has emphasised as the social, political and economic unit the group of adherents of each religion and has emphasised the distinction even the antagonism between such groups..."[4] It is a situation wherein communities tend to separate each other on the basis of membership in religious groups. In a broad sense "communalism is the belief that because a group of people follow a particular religion they have as a result of that fact common social, political and economic interest."[5] Exclusiveness tends to be the basic and fundamental ingredient of communalism. Religious groups are supposed to have distinctive interests. "As an ideology communalism refers to the belief that people belonging to one religion also share common socio-economic, political and cultural interests. As a social phenomenon it refers to an exclusive assertion justified in the name of a group in this context a religious group."[6] Such feelings tend to produce network for activations as action-sets to fulfil group goals. It seeks a classification of people on the basis of religion and tends to promote hostility and conflict. It represents a conflict of interest legitimised by religion and finds manifestation in the assertiveness of individuals. It is also defined as the functioning of religious communities or organisations which claim to represent them, in a way which is considered determinantal of other groups or of the nation as a whole.[7] In such a situation a religious group seeks "an exclusive political roof" for a secure existence.[8] Thus communalism is the political, economic and social assertiveness of an organised aggregation of individuals identifying themselves with a particular religious group. It is "essentially manipulation of social consciousness based on religion for political purposes."[9] Communalism is exploitation of religious identities to suit political interests. It triggers in its wake instincts disruptive to unity in diversity. Communalism is perverse form of secularism. It represents a process of "competitive desecularization involving re-sacralization of the nation space."[10] It is an orientation opposed to secularism and "has come to mean that consciousness which is prompted by one's belonging to a distinctive religious community."[11] In such circumstances religion ceases to be a personal affair as it is articulated to suit political and economic interests. It derives sustenance from an orientation for antagonism against other religious communities. It is an "organised political movement based on proclaimed interests of a religious community usually in response to a real or imagined threat from another religious community."[12]

II

Fundamentalism has been on increase especially during the recent years. Proclivity toward violence and disregard for democratic and human values is on increase. Parochial identities based on ethnic and religious alliances that characterise the new world order "is global in its scope, binary in its opposition and occasionally violent and essentially a difference of ideologies."[13] The societies of the third world are no exception to it. Faith as an identity has led to polarization of society on communal lines. Religion is in 'combustive association' with nationalism.

In India communalism is a dreaded legacy of the colonial past. Initiated by the British it soon penetrated deep to get itself embedded in the Indian society. "The history of Indian nationalist movement unfortunately is also a history of the communalisation of Indian society. That the colonial rulers actively encouraged and aided this process is undoubtedly true, but it was essentially a result of this weakness and inadequacy of secularism as conceived and perceived during the anti-colonial struggle."[14] Communalism has now acquired a pervasive existence. Political modernization and economic development accelerated its sweep and intensity. Society seethes with expressions of a vibrant religiosity. Communalism has acquired a permanent existence in India and has contributed large scale destruction of life and property. India has been witness to deadly spiral of violence in which many of its states remain terribly mired. Community specific identity has contributed to ethnicization of the society. Solidarity between religious communities is often impaired. Opposition to pluralism and egalitarianism is mounting. Communalism looms menacingly over much of India as secularism is reduced to an embattled ideology "no longer sanguine about its future."[15] The ideology of communalism has acquired a respectable location. Spectre of continued communal violence in the land of love and compassion is shocking indeed. "Not even the worst cynic could have expected the fruits of freedom to be so bitter and so sour. Not even the worst pessimist could have ever expected such naked dance of death and violence in a country which had produced the greatest apostle of non-violence and which had also been the laboratory of the greatest experiment."[16] The incidents of riots are increasing and these tend to be prolonged. Weakening of the ideology of secularism has led to "an increasing use of religion in the social construction of ethnic and communal identity which is made the basis for articulation of common economic interests and political mobilization."[17]

III

Politics seems to have strengthened religious and communitarian solidarities in India. Primordialities have been manipulated to seek political mileage. Faith as an identity has been exploited for political power. It has strengthened traditional instincts. Competitive communalism is indicative of the failure of the forces of modernization to ensure issue-oriented politics. Competition among political parties to secure electoral support has led them to resort to strategies that foster fundamentalism. Competitive communalism is thus an important fallout of the process of politicization. It is not "religious difference as such but its exploitation by calculating politicians for the achievement of secular ends which had produced the communal divide."[18] Communal mobilization suits the design of political parties in India. Religious affiliations have to be politicised for promotion of communal ideology. Selective appropriation and distorted interpretation of history lends sustenance to communalism. It has been the endeavour of the communal forces to exploit the historical antecedents of the communities to strengthen the pre-existing divide. In spite of identical socio-economic location the cleavages between the communities acquire escalation through a conscious process of symbol selection. Such sections of the society as have extra concern for preservation of identity turn themselves against the tide favouring evolution of the civic culture. Their urge for nativism is nurtured by elements exploiting their traditional identity for political ends. Communal strains occur in events of assertion of identities by competing communities. Conflicts tend to be intense where perceived damage to religious sentiment is high. Apprehension with regard to loss of identity often strengthens the inclination among the people for desperate clinging to the faltering tradition. In an economy of scarcity communalism manifests rather violently particularly in the wake of competition for share in the fruits of development. It acquires acute dimension, if it relates to activities that have been the exclusive province of a particular community. Then in such instances where recently acquired economic prosperity is used to ensure religious solidarity the chances for communalisation of the society are high. Fraternity across communal cleavages tends to be fragile even among the working classes.

IV

Local provocations lead to communal riots. Such areas are termed as areas primarily affected by communal violence. Issues leading to communal violence in such areas are of indigenous origin. Other cases represent an extension of tensions that have distant roots. There are occasions where secondarily affected areas turn out to be a transmission belt to instigate identical violence in far-off places. The base of communalism tends to be inclusive. It is no longer exclusive to the upper castes. It is also not a middle class phenomenon. There have been attempts to ensure the deep involvement of the poor and destitutes in promotion of religion-based violence and destruction. It has ceased to be spasmodic as it tends to be persistent. It appears that the so-called "modernised segment" of the society has not been weaned away from the hold of primordial feelings. It would also be interesting to note that the evidences of active participation of religious leaders in the communal clashes are few and far between. In the communal conflicts secular elites tend to be in command. Expression of communal instincts is no longer considered to be a matter of shame. Involvement in communal politics is often regarded prestigious. Communalists are no longer unacceptable in the society. Inhuman brutality is accorded legitimatization by elevating "a temporal struggle to the level of the cosmic."[19]

V

Riots are no longer an urban phenomenon. These have now ruptured the intimate matrix of relationship prevalent in the rural society. There are areas that are prone to communal violence. Cracks in communal solidarity are difficult to be repaired. Riots tend to be brutal as there has been an increased use of sophisticated deadly weapons. Violence acquires a familiar shape as it becomes frequent. Communal passions are instigated with the help of emotional issues. Retaliations are immediate, violent and directed. Outgroup hostility tends to strengthen ingroup solidarity. Symbols of religion like music before a mosque initiate riots in many cases. Such religious issues as cow slaughter or desecration of places of worship are no longer mentioned to be the reasons for outbreak of communal riots. In fact tension is reported to have been caused mostly over celebration of religious festivals. In such instances however religion is a camouflage as the real purpose is to ensure dominance of a particular community. In addition to the immediate factors there are many more contributing factors. Some tend to be transparent while many others remain disguised. While religion has a life of its own as primary determinant of communalism it operates in tandem with economic and political realities. In presence of incendiary materials not much is needed to cause a flareup. The immediate provocations constitute simply a match stick that set the haystacks on fire. The Muslims are the worst sufferers in the riots.

VI

State plays an important role in the communalisation of the society. The character of the regime is an important variable determining the extent and magnitude of communalisation of the society. Instable and weak regime tends to be ineffective on such occasions. Secular ideology is not sufficient in itself. It needs sincere and effective leadership for its actualisation. Administrative machinery in order to be effective has to be sensitive to the issues of communal harmony. Lapses on their part unleash unmanageable disaster. Secularism "depends on the quality of human agents on whom rests the responsibility of safeguarding the spirit of secularism through their policies and actions in different fields of national life especially at critical moments."[20]

REFERENCES

1. T.K. Oommen : *State and Society in India*, Sage Publications, New Delhi, 1990.
2. Sudipta Kaviraj : "Religion, Politics and Modernity" in *Crisis and Change in Contemporary India*, ed., by Upendra Baxi and Bhikhu Parekh, Sage Publications, New Delhi, 1995, p. 306.
3. Gyanendra Pandey : *The Construction of Communalism in Colonial North India*, Oxford University Press, Delhi, p. 6.
4. Wilfred Cantwell Smith : *Modern Islam in India*, Usha Publications, New Delhi, 1979.
5. Bipan Chandra, "Communalism : Misreading of Social Reality", *Mainstream*, May 31, 1980, p. 7.
6. Manoranjan Mohanty : "Communalism : A democratic rights' perspective", *Lokayan Bulletin*, Vol. 5, 1987, p. 58.
7. Donald E. Smith : *India as a Secular State*, Oxford University Press, 1963, p. 454.
8. T.K. Oommen, *op. cit.*, p. 112.
9. K.N. Panikkar : "Introduction" to *Communalism in India*, Manohar, New Delhi, 1991, p. 8.
10. Satish Despande : "Communalism in the Nation Space", in *Economic and Political Weekly*, Vol. 30, No. 50, 1995, p. 32.

11. Kumaresh Chakravarty : 'Towards a Genesis of the Recent Upsurge in Communalism' in *Communalism in India : Challenge and Response* (Ed.) by Mehdi Ahshan and Janki Rajan, Manohar, 1994, p. 11.

12. Gyanendra Pandey, *op. cit.*

13. Mark Juergensmeyer : *Religious Nationalism Confronts the Secular State*. Oxford University Press, New Delhi, 1994, p. 2.

14. K.N. Panikkar, *op. cit.*

15. Dipankar Gupta : 'Secularism and Minoritisation—Limits of heroic thought', in *Economic and Political Weekly*, Vol. 30, No. 35, September 1995, p. 2203.

16. P.C. Joshi : *Secularism and Development : The Indian Experiment*, Vikas Publishing House Pvt. Ltd., 1995.

17. Joseph Tharamanglam : "Indian Social Scientists and Critique of Secularism" in *Economic and Political Weekly*, Vol. 30, No. 9, 1995.

18. T.N. Madan : "Secularism in its Place' in *Religion in India* (ed.) by T.N. Madan, Oxford University Press, New Delhi, 1991, p. 398.

19. Mark Juergensmeyer : 'The Logic of Religious Violence' in *Religion in India* (ed.) by T.N. Madan, Oxford University Press, New Delhi, 1991, p. 383.

20. P.C. Joshi, *op. cit.*, p. 16.

6

THE PRACTICE OF SECULARISM

Acharya Rama Murti

I

I am a social worker, not a scholar. A social worker comes across certain problems whose solution requires persons with knowledge. To me you are such person. In my long life I have seen, in fact actually participated in a number of movements, namely, the national movement for freedom, Vinobaji's Bhoodan movement, and lastly J.P.'s Bihar movement. In the year 1946, in Varanasi during nights, the slogan people raised was : 'Allah-o-Akbar' (Muslim) which evoked the counter-slogan : 'Maro Salon Ko, Gandhiji Ki Jai'. The quarrel in those days was not between secularists and non-secularists. These words were used only in articles and serious writings. Frequent riots used to take place in those days. The terms in vogue were communalism and nationalism. The symbol of communalism was Mohd. Ali Jinnah and that of nationalism Mahatma Gandhi. Jinnah and British rulers were on one side. They had joined hands to frustrate Indian nationalism. After the riots of Kanpur in 1931, a committee was formed under the chairmanship of Dr. Bhagwan Das. It was known as 'Congress Kanpur Riots Enquiry Committee'. The committe prepared a report, the preface of which was an eye-opener for the public. It explained how British rulers made use of riots to weaken and defeat the National movement. For the first time people came to know that riots could also be used as an instrument for political objectives. The whole history of the period from 1944 to 1947 revolved round the fact that the British and the anti-nationalist forces like the Muslim League were on one side and the nationalist forces on the other. The Anglo-Muslim League forces ultimately won and India was divided. Conditions were created in which nationalists themselves were compelled to demand partition. I am mentioning this fact to show that in those days the word secularism was not used commonly but these days this word has become popular. Now perhaps the word nationalism is not in common use, and similarly, the word communalism too. The word secularism is in vogue. The expression 'Pseudo-secularist' is now a part of political vocabulary. These words cause confusion/complexities. The above terms are complex and if the minds of Hindus and Muslims have to be read, these terms have to be minutely analysed. It is worth mentioning that the Muslim community by and large has not forgotten that once they were conquerors and rulers. This feeling and memory took root since the times of Sir Sayyad Ahmed Khan. Muslims were told ultimately English rulers would leave this country and while departing, they would leave the same administrative set-up as is prevalent in England. In this system Hindus would be in overwhelming majority which would rule over the Muslim minority. Thus Muslims would become slaves to Hindus. This apprehension created fear in their minds. Jinnah played on this fear. In his meetings throughout the country Jinnah would ask Muslims : 'what will be your position after the departure of the English rulers? You will become slaves. It is the Hindus that will rule.' I wish to raise one question—why, in democratic set-up, the minority feels unprotected among majority and what is the remedy to get rid of this fear? In a secular country like India, what would be the place of minorities? This question is more political than religious. What would then be the shape of that democratic polity that frees the minorities from such fear? How should national and sub-national identities be integrated?

II

Fear of the majority rule is a challenge to secular polity, secular society, secular state. I will quote an example. It was the era of Bhindrawalla. Operation Blue Star had not taken place. I had an opportunity to go to Moga for a convention. A Gurudwara arranged our lunch. I was on my way to the Gurudwara when two young Sikhs came my way. In the course of our conversation I told them that Indian culture is a composite culture (Sangam Sanskriti), in which a number of streams mingle together. They appreciated the idea of composite culture. I was happy to note that at least they appreciated my idea. But they said that they could not accept it because they were followers of Bhindrawalla. I told the youth that in Punjab the proportion of Sikhs and Hindus is 52% and 48% respectively. What did they want in Khalsa Rajya? He said, 'Yes in Punjab we are in a majority but what about Delhi. We are condemned to Hindu Majority Rule for all times to come. We cannot accept this.' I thought that Muslims and Sikhs have similar fear—domination by Hindus. I will cite another example. After Biharsharif riots, I had the opportunity to visit a village in Nalanda (Bihar). In the evening while we were returning from a meeting we met a 60-year-old man who enquired of us as to whether we distributed land. I replied, Yes, provided we get land in gift. He enquired if he could get some land. I asked him, 'Are you landless?' His reply was, 'I am a farmer. I have ancestral land.' I then questioned, 'Then why are you asking for land?' He replied, 'There are only three families in this village belonging to my caste. Others belong to other castes. Although we are all Hindus yet I feel insecure, I wish to migrate to some other village in which my caste people are in a majority.' Again the same fear—majority domination. So long as this fear is there can there be co-existence of democracy, secularism in a vast and varied country like ours?

Being a social worker, a question arises in my mind as to how the co-existence of Hindus and Muslims and that of Dwijas and Shudras had been possible in this country for the last thousand years. There was much in common between Hindus and Muslims and between upper castes and lower castes. But the fact remains that there was much that separated the one from the other. This separateness has to go if India is to become a secular country. A secular state is not enough; we must have a secular society.

Let us see what Gandhiji thought about this question. Gandhiji said that he was a good Hindu as well as a good Musalman. DHARMA is not an organized religion. The essence of all the religions is the same. This was the view of King Ashoka also. Gandhiji called himself a *Sanatani* Hindu, as he believed in truth and non-violence which are eternal values. In the modern age, science comes very near truth and democracy is very much non-violence. Religion is the concern of the individual and not of any state or group. Nowhere in the inscriptions of Ashoka it is mentioned that he was a Buddhist.

Then what is the alternative of Hindu Rajya? The alternative is obviously *Bharatiya* rajya. Let every Indian be equal. Let the Constitution not permit conversion. The individual should be free to choose his religion. The law of the land should apply to all Indians equally. The Muslims did not accept the verdict of the Supreme Court in Shah Bano case. Why? Was she not an Indian citizen? When Syed Shahbuddin published a magazine 'Muslim India', many Hindus rightly asked, why Muslim India, why not Indian Muslim? This shows that nationalism, democracy, secularism should be redefined, federation should be restructured, and the Constitution should be suitably redrafted.

7

SECULARISM : THE CONCEPT AND PRACTICE IN INDIA

Vijay Kumar

Like equality, liberty and justice, 'secularism' is an elusive and confusing concept in the political lexicon. It is a protean, mutable concept which lacks precise definition but provides a convenient slogan for rallying ballot influence by the politicians. Words are, indeed, only tools for communication. Provided that we understand what other people mean when they use words, it is idle, unless we are writing a dictionary, to insist that one way of using the words is alone correct. And though a word like "secularism" may be descriptively ambiguous, it may have a prescriptive force of its own in the different contexts in which it is used.

The Concept

Though the concept of secularism does not find a place in the Encyclopaedia of Social Sciences, it is variously described in Encyclopaedia of Religion and Ethics and Encyclopaedia Britannica besides standard dictionaries. The Encyclopaedia of Religion and Ethics describes secularism as a term applied in general to the separation of state politics or administration from religious or church matters. It was a movement intentionally ethical, negatively religious, with political and philosophical antecedents.[1] The Encyclopaedia Britannica defines secular as 'non-spiritual, having no concern with religious or spiritual matters'. It is used in the wider sense of 'anything which is distinct, opposed to, or not connected with religion or ecclesiastical things, temporal as opposed to spiritual or ecclesiastical.'[2]

Though the concept of secularism is old and the West traces its origin to the beginnings of Christianity,[3] it emerged as an ethical and social movement in eighteenth century England. It was essentially a 'protest movement', an 'anti-religious reaction' against the "selfishness of the wealthy and influential classes, the unreasoning opposition to political and religious freedom, the stolid dogmatism of theology."[4] It was deeply influenced by the "asocialist" school of James Mill and Bentham with an "antitheistic strain inherited from Thomas Paine"[5] and by positivistic strain of G.H. Lewis and J.S. Mill.[6] Therefore, the British utilitarians may rightfully be called the forebears of secularism. However, its establishment and development as a politico-philosophical ideology was the handiwork of G.L. Holyoake and Charles Bradlaugh, particularly the former, who is often called the father of secularism.[7]

Secularism was a 'materialistic and rationalistic' ethical system which aimed at providing an alternative theory of life and conduct for those who had rejected Christianity. Like the 'end of ideology' it aimed at ushering in an era of 'end of religion'. It was not another religion but a philosophy based on the 'exclusion' of all religions. To the authors of secularism, it was not an alternative to religion, it was an alternative also to atheism. It did not seek to come into conflict with any religion and its tendency was agnostic—neither to deny nor to affirm the truth of religion or the existence of God. But later it acquired an atheistic bias.[8]

The secular movement reached its apogee in the middle of the nineteenth century coinciding with a period of anti-religious propaganda and then it rapidly declined and disappeared from independent existence. It lost its autonomous existence, merging into larger materialistic movements sweeping Europe.[9] However, its spirit survived in a variety of materialistic ideologies and movements with a bias to the exclusion of religion like scientific humanism, agnosticism, positivism, rationalism, intellectualism, existentialism, communism etc. Secularism, thus, in the West, inclines, according to Anson Phelps Stokes, "to hold religion in intellectual contempt, or to be at least indifferent to it and to assume that the state should give it no encouragement..."[10] Consequently, it is not surprising that secularism has been a constant butt of attack from religious quarters.

The Indian Scene

In India, the term secularism was not explicitly mentioned in the original constitution. It was inserted as an additional adjective before "republic" by the 42nd Constitutional Amendment Act during emergency. It is likely that the motive for the addition of the word "secular" like "socialist" was purely political. However, the Constitution of India guaranteed freedom of conscience, practice, profession and propagation of religion,[11] freedom to establish religious institutions and manage and administer their affairs, to hold, acquire and administer properties etc.[12] These rights are to be exercised in such a way as not to impair peace, order and social morality.[13] The Constitution prohibits discrimination on grounds of religion and guarantees legal and social equality to all providing for equality before the law and equal protection of the laws,[14] prohibiting discrimination with regard to places of public importance[15] and providing for equal opportunity in matters of public employment.[16] The Constitution further permits the religious minorities to conserve their script, language and culture[17] and allows them to establish and administer educational institutions of their choice.[18] These individual freedoms in the realm of religion undoubtedly make India a secular state even without the addition of the word in the Preamble. But even after forty years of the implementation of the Constitution, the Indian brand of secularism is clouded in confusion, misunderstanding and misinterpretation. Both Hindu and Muslim leaders feel that something is seriously wrong with secularism as preached and practised in India. Consequently, whenever there is communal tension, the very conception of secularism in India is questioned by all the people concerned. It is high time that all concerned sit up, rethink their thoughts and reexamine their basic assumptions about secularism. Otherwise, a strong feeling is building up in the minds of the ordinary people that all this talk about 'secularism', at least the political exploitation of the concept, has reduced it to simply a means for garnering minority vote. The much propagated bill on delinking religion from politics is also assumed to be a step in this direction.

Evaluating Indian Secularism

One thing that we have to keep in mind while evaluating the political concepts like secularism in the Indian political system is that Indian law, while resembling the forms of both American and British law in so far as protection of civil liberties is concerned, is somewhat alien to both of these systems. It reflects ancient Hindu and

Mohammedan influences that predate British colonial rule. A lengthy Constitution, which provides detailed descriptions of the powers of the government and rights of the people, shows concern for the difficult task of both governing a huge and diverse population and maintaining a democratic rule.[19] Since independence from British rule was achieved in 1947, Western observers have perhaps too readily predicted that India would have to adopt more authoritarian form of governmental leadership to overcome the pressures that threaten to tear the very system apart. It is, indeed, a tribute to indigenous stamina, nurtured by long cultural traditions, that India has found democratic forms and a tolerant attitude towards the right of her citizens desirable goals, when the crises of nation building might have tempted nations without the same moral resources and cultural traditions to turn openly towards dictatorship. Basic to this attitude is the fact that democracy was not introduced to India only in the last fifty odd years as Western institution. Rather democratic spirit existed for several centuries in the institutions of village *panchayats* and the ancient laws of *Dharmashastras*. The ancient law givers of the Hindus declared "*Sarvas sve sve grehe raja*" which means "every man is a king in his own house". Here one is tempted to recount the oft-quoted statement of B.R. Ambedkar that in India the "religious conceptions are so vast that they cover every aspect of life, from birth to death."[20]

Unlike the West, in India, secularism was not born out of the conflict between the Church and the state. It was rather infused by the spirit of religious tolerance developed during the long march of Indian civilization and culture. In India, where people from the moment of waking to the last moment of falling asleep, throughout the length and breadth of our land, are moved and motivated by faith, religious fervour and innate spirituality, secularism was not an absence or negation of religion or a strict adherence to the principle of absolute separation between state and religion. All it meant was religious impartiality, *Sarva Dharma Sambhava* i.e., treating all religions alike or giving equal respect to all religions instead of *Dharma Nirapeksha*, i.e., state neutrality in matters of religion.[21] If our secular state has nothing to do with religion then why does it conduct the elections of Sikh Gurudwara Prabandhak Committees or appoint Waqf Boards and Heads of Devasthans? Our secular state goes further. As an act of political patronage in the name of religion, it appoints politicians to head all these purely religious bodies. It even appoints ministers with these very portfolios.

Ideal Secularism

In an ideal sense, a secular state would imply the creation of non-interfering spheres of action for both state and religion. But in India it is not so, neither is it in any other state of the world. The first amendment to the U.S. Constitution articulates political and religious freedom. "Congress shall make no law..." is absolute in its wordings. Still it is not only subject to judicial interpretation but there have developed established qualifications to the primary freedoms.[22] Religious expression in Mexico has been limited by many constitutional provisions. Freedom of religion is provided, but it is limited to the practice of religion in home : within places of public worship religion is subject to government supervision.[23] However, when the President of the United States of America is sworn to office by taking his oath on the *Bible*, there are no difficulties by this symbolic act. Kenneth Wald in his book on *Religion and Politics in the United States* confirms that religion plays an important role in the US political process and decisions at the state level. The US support to Israel can be largely attributed to 'religious' factors, namely, the Jewish Lobby and diverse rules for abortion and divorce in different states of United States may be attributed to religious factor, viz., the proportion of Catholics in the population.[24]

The secular state is not expected to remain a neutral umpire in the religious game because religion can be used for various purposes other than ecclesiastical. Secularism has to grapple with organized religions of all kinds because basically it is an ideology—however an open ideology it may happen to be—in the given political culture of the society. It can always afford to remain indifferent to it.

In the Western democracies practice of secularism is easier in the sense that there is still a large homogeneity in religious affairs as compared to India. "Protestants and Catholics differ from each other roughly as much as does one Hindu caste from another. Christians and Jews differ perhaps as much as do Hindus and Jains, or Hindus and Buddhists..."[25] Still Christians have much to be ashamed of in their treatment of Jews. Lately, wherever there is a larger population of Muslims in Europe, Christians and Muslims have refused to live together as a nation despite secular outlook of Christianity. And though the concept of secularism was borrowed from the West, it never was intended to be anti-religious, agnostic or irreligious in India. In 1947 in his book *Religion and Society*, S. Radhakrishnan pointed out that "Secularism is the chief weakness of our age." In 1955 in his *Recovery of Faith*, he warned : "the religious impartiality of the Indian State is not to be confused with secularism or atheism.

Secularism as here defined is in accordance with the ancient religious tradition of India."[26] Obviously, what he meant to suggest was the Indian tradition of tolerance towards other religions and religious communities. He wrote in 1956 : "It may appear somewhat strange that our Government was a secular one while our culture is rooted in spiritual values."[27] Further, he goes on : "Secularism here does not mean irreligion or atheism or even stress on material comfort, it proclaims that it lays stress on the universality of spiritual values which may be attained by a variety of ways."[28] Mahatma Gandhi, though a man of religion, a Hindu to the innermost depth of his being, was extremely secular in his approach to religion. In 1928 he stated :

> "After long study and experience I have come to these conclusions, that: (1) all religions are true, (2) all religions have some error in them, (3) all religions are almost as dear to me as my own Hinduism. My veneration for other faiths is the same as for my own faith."[29]

It was this kind of secularism that was enshrined in the Indian Constitution. But in a country where the British policy of 'divide and rule' had created privileged enclaves, democratic and secular norms were difficult to develop. The new rulers had no compunction in following the values and principles of their colonial masters while framing the rules of the Constitution and diluting the indigenous values of the people under the high sounding western concepts of liberty, equality, justice, democracy, socialism and secularism. Nyerere was very apt when he pointed out that constitutional guarantees for the individual in a developing nation tend to defeat the very purpose for which they are set up, for they serve to protect those whose object is to subvert and destroy democracy itself.[30] The vested interests in India began to consolidate minorities and minorityism because consolidated minorities can be used against the majority which can be easily fragmented and rendered powerless. Secular principles which were an offshoot of Indian ethos and culture and were incorporated in the Constitution of the country which had just suffered partition on the basis of religion, become a spear directed against the heart of Hinduism which lays down no dogmas, punished no dissent, accepts the role of reason and promotes unhampered inquiry in all matters, spiritual and temporal. The Hindus never issued a *fatwa* because they always accepted the right to dissent.

Secularism in Practice

The most celebrated recent case of minorityism is that of Shah Bano. Whereas Article 44 of the Constitution directs the state to strive for a Uniform Civil Code for all citizens, the central government nullified the Supreme Court's decision to make the husband responsible for maintaining his divorced wife. If a constitution is secular, all citizens must be governed by the same laws in all matters of inheritance, marriage and allied matters because these are concerned with social sphere of life and not the realm of religion. Likewise, if compelling Hindus to be monogamous could be a measure of social reform, the fundamental right to religion could not stand in its way, the principle applies equally to Muslims and other minorities. It is the height of hypocrisy to claim to be a secularist and disown Article 44 at the same time. When an Islamic country like Pakistan could declare polygamy and instant *talaq* illegal during Ayub Khan's regime,[31] why can't this be done in a secular country like India? Then there are other unequal provisions in the Indian Constitution. Articles 29 and 30 allow minorities to get government grants to run their schools and colleges, and give religious instructions there. Hindus have been denied this right. Just to preclude governmental interference out of their schools, the Ramkrishna Mission was driven to declare itself a non-Hindu organization, much to the consternation of Hindus.[32] The idea behind Article 30 was to let minorities run their educational institutions to protect their linguistic and cultural heritage and identity. It was never meant to favour them in the matter of property rights or in the criteria for establishing their institutions. But the managements of minority institutions interpret this article to mean that while they are entitled to government grants, they are not subject to any governmental control or even guidance.[33] And this is what has precisely happened in the name of secularism in our country.

Conclusion

Separate provisions for different communities end up by creating walls between them. Vested interests grow which find it profitable to keep them apart. Keeping them apart not only prevents and blocks their entry in the mainstream but also perpetuates the stranglehold of the vested interests. It promotes fundamentalism and fanaticism. Secularism under the cover of protectionism becomes a social myth which draws a curtain over the failure of the minority to distinguish politics from religion in the society in which its members live. Secularism becomes a dream of the minority which wants to shape the majority in its own image, which is not practically possible in a liberal democratic set-up. The minority becomes a handmaid of politicians who use secularism as an instrument of permissive communalism rather than what can be called honest secularism of *Sarva Dharma Sambhava* which is the real essence of secularism.

REFERENCES

1. *Encyclopaedia of Religion and Ethics,* (ERE) articles on Secularism, Vol. 11, pp. 347-48.
2. *Encyclopaedia Britannica*, Vol. 20, p. 264.
3. V.M. Bachal, *Freedom of Religion and Indian Judiciary*, Poona : Shukhada Saraswati, 1975, p. 14.
4. *ERE.*
5. *Ibid.*
6. *Ibid.*
7. *Ibid.*
8. *Ibid.*
9. *Everyman's Encyclopaedia.*
10. Quoted in V.P. Luthera, "Religious Impartiality", *Seminar*, 67, March 1965, pp. 19-20.
11. Art. 25.
12. Art. 26.

13. Art. 25(1).
14. Art. 14.
15. Art. 15.
16. Art. 16.
17. Art. 29.
18. Art. 30.
19. M. Basu, *Introduction to the Indian Constitution*, New Delhi : Rejhi Publishing, 1960.
20. Constituent Assembly Debates, VII, 781.
21. Subhash C. Kashyap, "Difficulties of Defining Secularism", *Times of India*, 4-6-1993.
22. Fletcher N. Baldwin, Jr., "Constitutional Limitations on Government in Mexico, the United States and Uganda" in Richard P. Claude, ed., *Comparative Human Rights*, London : John Hopkins University Press, 1977, p. 80.
23. *Ibid.*, p. 81.
24. Kenneth D. Wald, *Religion and Politics in the United States*, New Delhi : Popular Prakashan, 1993.
25. W.C. Smith, "The Problem", *Seminar*, *op. cit.*, p. 10.
26. Quoted in Luthera, *op. cit.*, p. 21.
27. S. Radhakrishnan, 'Foreword' in S. Abid Hussain, *The National Culture of India*, Bombay : Jaico, 1956, pp. vii-viii.
28. *Ibid.*
29. M.K. Gandhi, *To the Hindus and Muslims*, Vol. III of the Gandhi Series Edited by Anand T. Hingorani, Allahabad : Law Journal Press, 1942, p. 412.
30. *Cf.* Baldwin, Jr., *op. cit.*, p. 84.
31. K.R. Malkani, "Parity and Partition : Corrosion Caused by Politicians' Secular Game", *Indian Express*, 10-4-1993.
32. K.R. Malkani, "Privileges for all groups", *Indian Express*, 21-6-1993.
33. *Ibid.*

8

COMMUNAL RIOTS AND ADMINISTRATION IN BIHAR

J. Narayan

Communal riots have become an integral feature of our social and political life. They occur very frequently; they claim more lives and property; and last much longer than before. Violent conflicts among different religious groups have become an important reality of the state.

In the name of communal riot it is the Hindu-Muslim conflict which is more concerning and demands greater and more urgent attention. Among the various forms in which conflicts between both the communities are expressed, riot stands out as the most obvious and alarming one. Bihar has had a long experience of Hindu-Muslim communalism and conflicts.

Communal riots generally occur at different places during Hindu as well as Muslim festivals. But in the past the main reason was the killing of 'Cow' by Muslims. Two very serious riots broke out at Koath in the sub-division of Sasaram in the district of Shahabad (now Rohtas) towards the end of August in 1893. During 1893-94 in Hilsa of Biharsharif and Basanpur of Gaya district serious riots took place. Some disturbances took place in the years 1911 and 1912 in the Monghyr and Patna districts. In 1915-16, serious riots broke out in the Patna district. The year 1917 particularly was marked by communal riots almost all over Bihar. Though the most serious and violent riot occurred in the Shahabad district and neighbouring districts of Gaya and Patna, the entire province had to bear the consequences of communal tension though in varying degrees. However, Shahabad, Gaya, Patna, Bhagalpur, Chotanagpur, Champaran and Sasaram proved more communally prone and riot-affected. Hence it would not be irrelevant to point out that the areas mentioned above had been important centres of either administration or religion during the Muslim period.[1]

Since Shahabad riot several communal incidents were witnessed by the state throughout the rest of the British phase. When the British were about to leave India, the country had to witness serious communal orgy.

Even after the creation of Pakistan we could not get rid of the virus of communalism. Rather it went on spreading fast. After independence with the introduction of democratic government based upon universal franchise, communalism acquired added value. Politics became highly communal and ethnicised in character. Caste, region, religion and language become the important idioms of Indian politics and provided support bases to political parties and their leaders. Naturally communalism became an important feature of the society and polity of Bihar.

Bihar has been a sensitive area from the communal point of view since long. Even after the creation of Pakistan most of the Muslims living here preferred to remain here and now they constitute a sizeable proportion of the population of Bihar. What is worth noting here is that their population has been increasing fast (Table 8.1).

Table 8.1 : Percentage Increase of Population of Hindus and Muslims in the Three Censuses of 1961, 1971 and 1981

	In 1961 over 1951			In 1971 over 1961			In 1981 over 1971		
	AC	H	M	AC	H	M	AC	H	M
All India	21.64	20.74	32.54	24.80	23.71	30.85	24.74	24.90	30.59
Bihar	19.76	18.96	32.29	21.30	19.54	31.26	24.06	22.34	30.03
Kerala	24.76	23.23	27.50	26.29	23.35	37.49	19.24	16.70	29.96
U.P.	16.66	16.13	19.48	19.79	18.52	26.77	25.49	24.82	29.11
W. Bengal	32.80	32.63	36.48	26.87	25.75	29.76	32.70	21.37	29.55

Note : AC—All Communities, H—Hindus, M—Muslims.

Besides this, the region has always been a centre of interest for Muslims as it has several monuments of historical as well as religious importance for them particularly, at Biharsharif, Patna (Phulwarisharif), Sasaram, Gaya and Bhagalpur.[2]

Bihar is one of the states where influx of Pakistani and Bangladeshi nationals and their resettlement have been a regular phenomenon although none of the districts of Bihar touches the boundary of Bangladesh. Yet it is only 18 kms from Kishanganj, a district of Bihar. The abnormal increase in Muslim population in recent years in the areas adjacent to the borders of Bangladesh may be attributed to gradual but constant influx of population from Bangladesh. Particularly the Bhatia Muslims have in large numbers infiltrated into the bordering areas. This has been possible mainly because of local Muslims' anxiety and role to increase their population. In these areas several atrocities have reportedly been committed by the Bangladeshi infiltrators in collusion with the local Muslims.[3]

Keeping these developments in view, Vishwa Hindu Parishad (VHP) chose to organise its congregation in 1982 at Kishanganj of Bihar. It was followed by the World Islamic Conference held at Araria in 1984 near Kishanganj. Another World Islamic Conference is now being held in Bihar at Gaya (2-4 September 1993). Just after that a three-day "Yuva Shakti Sammelan" under the banner of Bajrang Dal, a militant wing of Vishwa Hindu Parishad (V.H.P.), was held at Katihar in October-November 1993. Thus Bihar has been in the thick of communal activities and has provided a platform as broad as it can be anywhere for communalists to launch their operations.

By now six major communal riots have occurred after 1947 at different places at different times in Bihar, i.e., Ranchi-Hatia (1967), Sursand (1967), Jamshedpur (1979), Biharsharif (1981), Bhagalpur (1989) and Sitamarhi (1992). They were major in terms of their intensity, duration and implications.

These communal riots have exposed the role of our administration more than anything else. We find that it failed to apprehend the situation and even after the occurrence of a communal incident it failed to contain that immediately, which resulted in heavy losses of life and property and further strained relations between the two communities.

As far as the Ranchi-Hatia Riot (1967) was concerned, the local administration committed several acts of omission and commission during the riot. It turned a deaf ear to the information furnished by the Special Branch of Police, Ranchi district, in which apprehension of clashes between the two communities had been expressed and even to the wireless message of the Political (Special) Department of the Government of Bihar in which directions had been given to take precautionary measures in view of anti-Urdu agitation. It also failed to apprehend local goondas as a precautionary measure which was very essential for maintaining peace there. It even failed to check the wave of rumours which ultimately proved fatal to the peace in the region.[4]

Having seen the Ranchi-Hatia riot, officers at higher levels, particularly district levels, directed their subordinates at all levels to take extra precautionary measures on the occasion of festivals. But in spite of these instructions the local administration at Sursand did not take adequate precautions. The failure of administration to apprehend the impending trouble and take adequate precaution helped the situation deteriorate further. Moreover, there was also lack of coordination between the S.P., and the D.M. The most disturbing thing that appeared during the riot was that the integrity and impartiality of many officers including the S.P., was not above suspicion.

Similarly, the administration at Jamshedpur could not rise to the occasion when the Ram Navami festival was being celebrated and hence a much more serious and devastating riot at Jamshedpur in the year 1979. First, it failed to resolve the dispute regarding the route of Dimna Basti Akhara in time which was one of the important factors said to have surcharged the atmosphere of entire Jamshedpur communally since a year preceding the incident. Secondly, the administration centred its operations around one community, i.e., Hindu without properly assessing the mind of the other community and its preparations for organised violence. Thirdly, apprehending disturbances the D.C., had directed the local administration to apprehend anti-social elements and criminals, but the local administration failed to act accordingly. It nabbed only one Muslim criminal whereas it arrested as many as 137 Hindus said to be bad characters. It shows that the local administration did not apprehend trouble from the Muslim community. Fourthly, the local administration including Intelligence Department completely failed to sense the gravity of the situation. Fifthly, superior officers also failed in their assessment of preparations of local administration for the occasion. And finally, lack of coordination between the army and the administration as also among different wings of administration was visible on many occasions during the riot.[5]

So far as the Biharsharif Riot (1981) is concerned, the Balasubramanium Inquiry Commission accused the administration of its utter failure and even passed severe strictures on the D.M. and the S.P. of Nalanda district for concocting evidence to absolve themselves of their responsibilities during the riot.[6] Among administrative lapses the most glaring was the failure of the C.I.D., wing of the Police Department to apprehend the impending trouble. The police at the local level was lethargic and complacent. The administration also failed to apprehend rumour-mongers and anti-social elements in time.

The Bhagalpur Riot (1989), one of the biggest and bloodiest communal riots in recent memory, also tells the story of the failure of administration. The then Union Home Minister, Buta Singh, himself admitted that the Bihar Government failed to control the communal riots in spite of apprehension expressed by the Central Government earlier.[7]

It was pointed out that the district administration did not sense the situation in advance and unwisely allowed the *Ramshila* (sacred bricks to be used in the construction of Sri Ram Temple in Ayodhya at a disputed site) procession to pass through the Muslim locality. But it did not take the necessary steps for its peaceful progress. Nor did it apprehend anti-social elements or nab agent provocateurs. There were too few policemen around when stones and bombs rained on the procession. Curfew was declared at 5 p.m. on October 24, but it was enforced only after 2 p.m. the following day.[8]

Lack of coordination between the police and the administration was also one of the important reasons of administrative failure. When the then Union Home Minister, P. Chidambaram, directed the district administration to put the entire police force of the state deployed in Bhagalpur under the command of army, the Regional I.G., and the D.I.G., were reluctant to delegate their powers to the army. The Special District Magistrate A.K. Singh's orders too were not implemented seriously.[9]

The recent Sitamarhi riot broke out on 6th October, 1992. That was the last day of Durga Puja. The failure of administration was evident here also. Lack of coordination between the police and the civil wing did, in fact, contribute tremendously to the worsening of the situation. This is clear from the allegations and counter-allegations levelled by the police and civil administration against each other. The police blamed the civil administration for not going into the details of their report of an impending communal clash in Sitamarhi during Dashehra. Home Commissioner, Jiya Lal Arya, on the other hand, held the police responsible for the lapse. He said that no warning about a possible riot had come. This tug of war actually left the state in limbo and created an impression that nothing tangible could be done by the police or civil administration. The pity is that even the C.M. does not have much confidence in his policemen or even the administration.[10]

The above analysis reveals administrative failure but this is just only one side of the picture. The main question is why the administration fails to rise to the occasion. It is worth noting that administration sometimes feels demoralised due to the undue pressure of the politicians in power, which adversely affects the morale and functioning of the administration particularly during communal violence.

The police have been demoralised since independence. It was probably because of the fact that notice was taken of complaints by the people in general against them. During the British days the police was creating hatred among the people against itself by its own action. Since then we have not done anything to bridge that gulf between the police and the public. People are no more afraid of police.[11]

Moreover, certain steps taken by the government immediately create an unenviable position for the police especially. The United Front (U.F.) Government took over on the 5th of March, 1967. Within eight hours of the formation of the new U.F. Government, new cabinet held a special meeting on the evening of the 5th March and ordered a judicial inquiry into Patna police firing on January 5th and into the student-police clash at Ranchi on January 3rd. At the same time the Bihar Cabinet also ordered immediate release of all political prisoners and students arrested during the previous year in connection with political agitations. It also ordered withdrawal of cases pending against them and cancellation of warrants of arrest.

In this connection the statement of the then Chief Secretary of the Government of Bihar is worth noting. He said :

> The withdrawal of cases against the students including cases in connection with the abnormal educational agitations tended to dampen the morale of the police and magistracy.[12]

This is more clear from the statement of the then Inspector General of Police, Bihar. He stated before the Inquiry Commission :

> The Judicial Commissions of Inquiry were ordered after executive probes into these firings had justified the conduct of the officers. The officers felt that the inquiries are mostly ordered under pressure of the public and not so much on merit, or for political considerations. They further feel that they are at a great disadvantage in presenting their cases before these commissions.[13]

In the case of the Bhagalpur riot also we find active political interference which is apparent from the transfer of S.P. Dwivedi just after the outbreak of the riot. It so happened that he was once transferred but his transfer was stayed. Again, he was transferred.[14]

At Sitamarhi some trouble started on October 2, four days before the communal jolt. The police arrested the miscreants but on the intervention of some local politicians released most of them.[15] And then clashes broke out again on the question of immersion of the idol of Durga into the river. The communal fire subsided only after following tough administrative measures under the direct supervision of the C.M., the imposition of curfew and deployment of the Rapid Action Force.[16] A seven-member fact-finding team of the Bihar Pradesh Congress Committee which visited the riot-affected areas in Sitamarhi accused the administration of its lapses. Citing an example of administrative and police lapses they said that the police posted at Manjhaura in Riga could have prevented rioters had their rifles not misfired at the critical moment. They further said that two of the four rifles available with a posse of homeguard jawans were defective and hence could not be triggered off. Even the other homeguard jawans who used the rifles, the Committee pointed out, were so ignorant of the shooting that they missed all the targets.[17] Thus administrative lapses and lack of prudence on the part of local politicians were mainly responsible for the eruption of riots at Sitamarhi.[18]

The foregoing analysis reveals that the administration does not have a competent machinery to apprehend impending trouble well in advance. Keeping in view the enormity of the threat to communal peace and harmony, it can be said that it is badly ill-equipped. There is also lack of coordination among different authorities dealing with communal disturbances which also impedes its effectivity. Sometimes administration, too, acts in a partisan manner favouring one community against the other. Besides all these facts, administration suffers from some sort of demoralisation caused by the partisan attitude of the party in power and its frequent interferences in its functioning. In such circumstances it is unable to take strong preventive steps including arrest of suspects in advance. It appears that no one has learnt any lesson from these incidents.

REFERENCES

1. Mathur, Y.B., *Muslims and Changing India*, Trimurti Publications, New Delhi, 1972, pp. 2-4; also see Sarkar, J. Narayan, "Economic Life in Early Mediaeval Bihar (1206-1526)" in Askari, H.S. *et al.* (eds.), *The Comprehensive History of Bihar*, II (i), K.P.J.R. Institute, Patna, 1983, pp. 445-46.

2. Askari, H.S. *et al.* (eds.), *op. cit.*, pp. 445-46.

3. Daftuar, A.K., "The Laxmipur Carnage", *Occasional Papers*, A.N.S.I., of Social Studies, Patna, 1986.

4. Narayan, Jitendra, *Communal Riots in India : A Case Study of an Indian State*, Ashish Publishing House, New Delhi, 1992, p. 69.

5. Narayan, Jitendra, *op. cit.*, pp. 130-31.

6. Ghose, S.K., *Communal Riots in India : Meet the Challenge Unitedly*, Ashish Publishing House, New Delhi, 1987, p. 130.

7. *Navbharat Times*, Patna, 28 Oct., 1989.

8. *The Telegraph*, Calcutta, 2 Nov., 1989.

9. *The Hindustan Times*, Patna, 31 Oct., 1989.

10. *Frontline*, Madras, 6 Nov., 1992, p. 10.

11. *Report of the Commission of Inquiry on Communal Disturbances—Ranchi-Hatia, 1967*, Govt. of India, Ministry of Home Affairs, New Delhi, 1968, p. 94.

12. *Ibid.*, p. 95.
13. *Ibid.*, p. 94.
14. See Narayan, Jitendra, *op. cit.*, p. 174.
15. *Frontline*, *op. cit.*, p. 4.
16. *Ibid.*, p. 9.
17. See *The Times of India*, Patna, 15 Oct., 1992.
18. See *The Times of India*, Patna, 11 Oct., 1992, p. 12.

9

SECULARISM, RELIGION AND POLITICS

With Special Reference to Bihar Political System

Ravindra Kumar Verma

Introduction

Recent incident of Ayodhya (December 6, 1992) and proposed bill on separation of religion from politics have generated debates afresh on the nature of Indian State in terms of its being a secular polity. Although the issue was raised in the Constituent Assembly and need of a secular state was visualised but the term 'secular' was not included in the Constitution even after considerable discussions. After twenty-five years, in 1974 it was Mrs. Gandhi's Government which ventured to add 'secular' in the Preamble of the Constitution through 42nd Constitutional Amendment Bill. However, inclusion of a term in the Constitution could not make any significant change in state-craft particularly in terms of practice of secularism, secularism as we commonly perceive.

The practice of secularism in India has been alleged to be sometimes 'minorityist' and sometimes 'majorityist'. Not only this, each side has been taking its own view to interpret secularism by justifying its stand. The controversy has again taken its course afresh in the present situation. Political and electoral prospects owing to either secularism or communalism or 'cultural nationalism' have made the political actors (specially political parties and power-seekers) more involved these days. In the given situation a question arises—what is secularism and what is the nature of Indian polity? Do we perceive 'secularism' in the same way as do the Westerners? What is the place of religion in politics in India? India is a peculiar society and a polity. It is composed of people of various religions, hardly a religion in the world which does not exist in India with its own existence. However, the two major religious components of Indian society—the Hindus and the Muslims—are the main confronting communities. Communal riots between these two communities have been taking place from time to time. History of such riots dates back to the birth of Indian republic in modern times. The State of Bihar has been one of the worst hit states in India. Riots of Bhagalpur, Biharsharif, Ranchi and Sitamarhi are the recent examples in the State. Political actors and the state-craft have to play roles in establishing communal harmony in such situations. In view of practice of secularism, a question comes up—how do the political actors behave during communal outbreak and during electoral and general conditions? Another important point to ponder is the place of religion in a secular polity like India and Bihar and the limits of state action in dealing with religion-relating matters.[1]

In view of the above theoretical queries and quest in practice of secularism, the paper intends to examine the concept of secularism in general and in Indian context in particular and politics of Bihar in context of communalism and secularism and treatment meted out to the minority and majority communities by political parties both in power and in opposition.

Secularism—The Concept

The concept of secularism rests on the citizen's relationship with two abstract super entities—the God and the State. Both these entities wield power from the people or citizens. Thus their relationships determine the nature of State. The relationships can be seen in three ways: Firstly, the jurisdiction of religion comes in between the citizen and the state. In other words, religion (or the clergyman) has superiority over state-craft. Secondly, the state or Government has superiority over religion (or the clergyman). And thirdly, the state has no jurisdiction over the religion or clergyman and *vice-versa*. The third situation is perceived in Western countries as the secular nature of the State. The evolution of church-state relationship in Christian countries leaned, with the passage of time, towards secularity owing to political and religious confrontational situations.[2] In case of uniform religion in a Christian polity the state-craft had no difficulty in identifying the interest of church and the state. But with rise of multiplicity of religions and intra-religious sects, the state's role became difficult. Enforcement of any one sect (such as Catholic or Protestant) or creed would have led to the disruption of the peace and order of the society. Under these circumstances there was a tendency towards mutual tolerance. This is why most of the contemporary European philosophers argued against the enforcement of any religion by the state on its subjects. Bodin argued that where two or more religions already existed in a state, imposing religious uniformity was 'useless and worse than useless'. It (imposing religious uniformity) would merely lead to civil war and weaken the state. The interest of peace was greater than religious considerations.[3] The welfare state has obligation to render goods and restrain sufferings to the masses, hence to maintain peace and order.

As such the concept of secularism originated at a time when state demanded allegiance to it from its citizens in their religious life. Its aim was to safeguard the freedom of the church by taking the religious sphere out of the sphere of the state.[4] These two spheres are supreme in their affairs and both are free from bilateral interference in the regulation of matters like doctrine, dogma, laws, organisation, administration and discipline. However, it is to be cautious that the freedom of both these sovereigns should not restrict each other's sovereignty. The state and religion should impose limits for themselves in order to maintain non-interference. Thus in the secular nature of a state, any religion is not to be promoted by state. Such state is not to give financial aid, large or small, direct or indirect, to any religious organisation or religious activities. On the other hand religion should not be made a public business.[5]

Here comes the individual citizen who has an absolute freedom of conscience, but his right to the practice of his religion, by its very nature, is to be exercised within the framework of the laws of the state. Thus the supremacy of state is bound to be there for ordering the individual's behaviour particularly in context of his religious activities, no doubt, except his religious faith and feelings.

The secularism as discussed above, thus, means that state has no roles to play in management of religious affairs. Although the religious groups are part and parcel of the state, yet the state-craft keeps itself away from the religious matters in a state having secular nature. It happened so owing to two basic factors—interests of various religious groups intersecting among themselves and secondly, these religious groups were organised and had been enjoying political power or hegemony over the state before secularism took place. But for India, secularism is not the instrument to mitigate the 'state-religion conflict' but it is instrument of 'communal harmony' and 'communal tolerance'. Thus, in Indian context, secularism guarantees individual and corporate freedom of religions, deals with individual as a citizen irrespective of his religion, is not constitutionally connected to a religion nor does it seek either to promote or interfere with it. Radhakrishnan also said, "secularism meant non-communalism."[6] This will be proved in the lines to come.

Secularism—Nature and Practice

If secularism means separation of state and religion or religious bodies, then Indian state has some different nature from what exactly it is called secularism as in Western Christian countries. Luthera, although argues that Indian state is not 'theocratic', strongly advocated that it is not even a secular state. He further goes on to say, "The fact is that it is neither possible nor desirable to have secular state in India... The secularisation of the state means its separation from religion and the consequent independence of religious bodies from the control and regulation by the state of their internal affairs."[7] He feels that the majority religious group 'Hinduism' is not organised in the same manner as Church in Western world. Hence there has been immense interference of the state in the management of religious matters in India. The Indian state can 'give direct or indirect financial aid to religious institutions'. It can enact communal legislation applicable differently to different religious communities. It can make religion a ground for discrimination among or classification of citizens. Luthera brands Indian state as a jurisdictionalist state.[8] The great Indian philosopher Dr. Radhakrishnan has also opined that the religious impartiality of the Indian state is not to be confused with 'secularism' or 'atheism'. It tries to build up a fellowship of believers not by subordinating individual qualities to the group mind but by bringing them into harmony with each other.[9] Luthera tries to articulate the nature of Indian state in a simple term, "it would perhaps be appropriate to describe it as a 'religiously impartial' or 'non-communal' state."[10] On examination of certain arguments in the Constituent Assembly, one can perceive this proposition. Chaudhri Ranbir Singh opined "our object of establishing a secular state in this country would remain merely an unrealized dream if we decide to provide safeguards on grounds of religion."[11] Another argument was placed by Loknath Mishra, who had doubts about divorce of religion from life. "By secular state, as I understand, is meant that the state is not going to make any discrimination whatsoever on the ground of religion or community against any person professing any particular form of faith. This means, in essence, that no particular religion in the state will receive any state patronage whatsoever."[12] "I do not mean to say that a state should be anti-religious or irreligious. But to my mind, a secular state is neither a Godless state nor an irreligious nor an anti-religious state."[13] One more argument says, "In a secular state...the state is expected to view all denominations in the same light and not give encouragement to any one particular denomination at expense of others."[14]

The Constitution of India has conferred on to its citizens the right to pursue religious beliefs and practices in full freedom as reflected in Articles 15, 16, 25, 26, 28, 29 and 30 of the Indian Constitution. As such the Constitution also envisaged a 'non-communal state' for India. However, the Constitution has allowed the Government to take measure to protect the interest of minority religions in order to maintain communal harmony and it did by setting up minorities commission, by launching Fifteen-Point Programmes for Welfare of Minorities (in 1983) and also by establishing a National Integration Council. Even then communalism has been flourishing in this country owing to the reasons like dubious role played by political parties, rise of fundamentalism, interference by foreign powers and 'weak-kneed' policy of Government.[15] In fact we needed and it is also feasible in our polity that a 'non-communal' state or a state having commitment to communal harmony should be established, nevertheless we call it a 'secular policy', secularism of Indian nature. The plurality of religions in India and various religious groups with minority population need to be paid state's attention for protection of minority groups. Nevertheless, there has been heartening reaffirmation, in the post-independence politics, of country's abiding faith in a secular modern India. However, communalism of one variety or another has always been a major issue in Indian politics and elections. In the past, expressions of communalism in the majority community were never so salient that political parties could not cope with them through their usual electoral strategies. Now Hindu communalism has emerged as a national sentiment. Similarly, minority communalism was handled in the past by couching minority demands in language of equity, welfare and development. These days language of minority communalism is no longer one of acquiring economic opportunities within the framework of pluralist democracy but it is of political autonomy and power. The practice of secularism in India has been involving, thus, three issues—minorityism, majorityism and place of religion in politics. The first issue is that of appeasement of the fundamentalist leadership of the minority community—the Muslims, which we call 'minorityism'. Such steps do not influence the day-to-day lives of the common people. This has not made the Muslims and other minorities more prosperous. However, these steps have, no doubt, strengthened the fundamentalist leadership.[16] Secondly, on the other hand this has made Hindus to react and prepare for similar treatment. Certain political parties foresee prospects in elections by pushing up the Hindu fundamentalists on the political front. As Hindus are in majority, such political parties are mobilising political support in the name of 'cultural nationalism' or secularism of majorityist nature commonly perceived as 'majorityism'.

In the absence of any local relevance secularism has come to mean different things to different men. The Muslims think they have something special in secularism, the Hindus resent that Muslim should get a Lollipop called secularism. In other words, fundamentalism arises out of insecurity not assurance. There is a outburst of fundamentalism in all religions today because we have entered an age of a new insecurity.[17] Thirdly, 'Majorityist' and 'Minorityist' styles of secularism have brought the religion in sharp confrontation to politics. In other words, the question relates to place of religion in politics. What we see today is the culmination of a phase of Indian politics in which the use of religions, and in fact communal means was overlooked as long as it led to political power.[18] The movement launched for a Hindu Rashtra, as a study finds out, is not a spontaneous movement but "a meticulously organised effort... This is indeed a complex phenomenon because majority communalism has got the advantage of projecting it as national."[19]

Religion Vs. Politics

In the wake of majority communalism, the Government led by Narasimha Rao ventured to throw up an anti-religious legislation but its wide unacceptability made him to drop the bill. The bill attracted a large number of critics from the intelligentsia. Veteran political scientist S.R. Maheshwari wrote, "The bill on religion was ill-advised and ill-conceived. It would have opened the floodgates of legal wrangles... Religion is component of Indian psyche and no one, not at least in India, can keep it away. It cannot be denied its due place in the political life... Law alone cannot wean politics from religion."[20] T.N. Pandey questioned its feasibility and remarked, "such legislation is not prompted by any avowed values in public life but merely to achieve a political goal." Examining its provisions he fears that it would give a lethal blow to the democratic system in the country. He concludes, "Hence the need is to delink corruption from politics not religion."[21] Rajeev Dhavan is scared that it might cause damage to Indian electoral system and argues, "Electoral democracy will get caught in cobwebs of fratricidal party politics... The bills are a conspiracy against people. Meanwhile, communalism must be countered at people's level".[22] Ashgar Ali Engineer brands the bill as 'perhaps worse than remedy'. He further advocates, "...if secularism does not strike firm roots among the people, the politicians can find out various ways of flouting even the strictest law."[23] Engineer suggests three strategies to tackle the problem in which religious tolerance is an important strategy.

The discussion takes us to the conclusion that religion is part of life and as such cannot be separated from political sphere, particularly, at least through enacting laws. The critics have one common thing to advocate that the problem of communalism should be solved not at political level rather at social level. In fact the history of Indian society has a tolerant streak in its communal relationships. Both the communities in India are interdependent in many spheres such as—the economy, the local polity, the social relationships, problems faced with Government machinery, the natural resources and so on except the faith.

Bihar Political System

The Bihar political system is not exception of Indian social and political texture but it has been different in secular behaviour. As regards the texture, the following is the population distribution according to religions as per 1981 census (1991 census report does not reveal the religion-wise population distribution) :

Population Distribution by Religion

Religions/ Community	Total Population	Percentage to total population	Growth rate (1971-81)
1	2	3	4
Hindus	5,80,11,070	82.97	23.34
Muslims	98,74,993	14.13	30.03
Christians	7,40,186	1.06	12.37
Sikhs	77,704	0.11	26.31
Jains	27,613	0.04	9.64
Buddhists	3,003	Negligible	37.52
Others	11,79,878	1.69	22.77

Source : Census of India 1981.

All communities, of course, the Hindus and the Muslims have intra-community divisions in them. Caste factor in Hindu community is though prominent, the Muslim community has also social divisions like forwards and backwards (the Pathans and the Momins). They constitute one-eighth of the total electorate, and are relatively homogeneous and capable of acting *en bloc* at the micro and macro levels. This makes their voting behaviour and political significance more prominent.[24] The Muslims have produced important leaders from Bihar like Hasan Imam, Ali Imam, Mazharul Haque, Abdul Bari and many others. They were stalwart freedom fighters. Bihar Muslims were not very active in propaganda for the two-nation theory and Pakistan.[25] In post-independence period among many Muslim leaders contributing to the political and social mainstream of Bihar are Azfan Imam, Abdul Quaum Ansari (Momin leader), Abdul Gafoor, Tarique Anwar, Gulam Sarwar, etc. These leaders never propagated fundamentalism and fanaticism in Bihar politics.

In 1947 the riots in the state were a sequel to the atrocities perpetrated on the Hindus of Noakhali.[26] All the riots that have taken place in post-1947 era in Bihar were instigated by anti-social elements,[27] no doubt, the political parties always utilised them for electoral gains. The report of the commission examining riots at Jamshedpur observed that "the R.S.S., with its extensive organisation in Jamshedpur had a positive hand in creating a climate which fostered the outbreak of the communal disturbances and singled out the names of RSS chief and a BJP M.L.A. of Bihar for inciting violence."[28] In another case of Biharsharif the communal riots burst out on the issue of a dispute of temple land. Besides, the Enquiry Commission's report stated that the violence in Biharsharif was a result of administrative failure of district administration. The Commission also said, "there was no implementation of the Government instruction that in a communal emergency rumours must be effectively scotched. On the other hand it was argued that the administration does not operate in vacuum and is scarcely neutral or unaffected by the communal or other socio-cultural divides. And specially after the Moradabad riots this has been important to bear in mind."[29] The Bhagalpur riots were also the outcome of slack district administration, specially the executive officer on the spot. Ashok Singh who enquired the Bhagalpur riots has also in his report blamed the Magistrate posted on spot for his inactiveness and dereliction of duty.[30] Thus here we come to the conclusion that the outbreak of Hindu-Muslim riots in Bihar has been instrumented by the anti-social elements and careless administration and the political parties fish out of the troubled water.

The State Government has, since independence, been adopting the appeasement policy for the minority leadership and been taking measures like liberally releasing funds to institutions and organisations of minority community, declaring Urdu as second state language, providing greater share in public offices, setting up Minorities Commission, announcing government jobs for them and so on. In other words, special care has been taken in favour of minority community by the State.

The BJP, alleged to be Hindu fanatist party, although less effective in Bihar, has been behaving (particularly after Ayodhya issue 1990) in a communalist manner. The 'Rath Yatra' led by L.K. Advani turmoiled the social order in the midst of already grave situation in Bihar owing to Mandal phenomena. Riots did not occur during 'Rath Yatra' because of alert J.D. workers from Hindu community on behest of the Chief Minister Laloo Prasad Yadav. The Ministers of his party were sent in their constituencies to check the expected violence. The Muslims were provided special protection by the State. The deadlock situation created by razing down the disputed structure (Babri Masjid Ram Janam Bhoomi) at Ayodhya on 6 December, 1992 was tackled intelligently by the Bihar Government. The communal riots although burst out at few places including Lohardagga, its intensity was lesser than that of other parts of the country. The Sitamarhi riots broke out on the 7th October, 1992. But the Chief Minister himself with various ministers was working at Sitamarhi to establish communal harmony. Not only this, the State Government set up special court for disposal of Sitamarhi riot cases. This was probably the first time in the judicial history of the country that all procedure of investigation, submission of chargesheet, conclusion of trial and delivery of judgement was completed within the period of about a year.[31] However, the steps taken by State Government (in post-1990 period too) were inclined towards minority community. The reason might be fanatical tendency of the BJP in Bihar.

As Rajani Kothari[32] strongly propounds that communalism is the child of electoral politics, the electoral behaviour of political parties in context of practice of communal harmony must be examined. As such fielding the members of different communities in the election fray by different political parties may depict certain trends.

Religionwise Percentage of Electoral Candidates
(Lok Sabha Elections 1989 and 1991)

Parties/ Communities	Share in Population (Percentage)	J.D.		Cong. I		BJP		SJP*
		1989	1991	1989	1991	1989	1991	1991
Hindus (including SC/ST)	82.97	89.2	76.5	88.9	88.9	98.2	98.2	78.4
Muslims	14.13	8.1	21.7	11.1	11.1	-	-	21.6
Others	2.90	2.7	1.8	-	-	1.8	1.8	-
Total	100.0	100.0	100.0	100.0	100.0	100.0	100.0	100.0

*SJP did not exist in 1989.

The above figures suggest that the BJP in Bihar provided tickets to Hindus (98.2%) and Christians (1.8%) in the name of minority representation and ignored the biggest minority community—the Muslims. On the other hand the Janata Dal provided tickets to all communities but giving greater premium on Muslim community. All the parties have given tickets to different communities disproportionate to their share in population. However, JD raised the percentage sizeably in case of Muslims as compared to 1989 Lok Sabha elections.[33] The election results may also throw light on the people's response to the political parties communitywise.

Religionwise Percentage of Total M.Ps. (L.S.) from Bihar
(A Comparison Between 1989 and 1991)

Parties/	J.D. and Others		Cong. I		BJP		Total	
Communities	1989	1991	1989	1991	1989	1991	1989	1991
Hindus including ST/SC	66.7	72.9	5.5	1.8	16.7	10.4	92.7	85.3
Muslims	3.7	12.3	1.8	—	—	—	5.5	12.5
Others	1.8	2.1	—	—	—	—	1.8	2.2

The figures speak for themselves. The share of Muslim minority in political system in the state has increased in post-1990 period coming to nearly in proportion of their share of population. For this the credit goes to Janata Dal. In conclusion, we can posit that the minority communities must be provided proper economic, political and social opportunities, otherwise the feeling of insecurity will grow, thereby breeding separatism and communalism. On the other hand the behaviour of political actors should be conducive to true secularism, rather communal harmony and good should be rendered to masses not in order to appease the fundamentalist leaders of either minority or majority communities but to provide due economic and political opportunities to the communities.

The political parties, in view of electoral prospects, try to attract the Muslim religious leaders in their favour. On the other side the Muslim religious leaders have been issuing statements and *Fatwa* to cast vote in favour of certain party(ies). This is the situation of bilateral interference of religion and state. Here it is to be examined how do the Muslim leaders of political parties behave vis-a-vis Muslim religious leaders? In present Assembly elections (1993) the

Imam of Jama Masjid warned the non-Congress and non-BJP parties to unite, otherwise they would not get Muslims' vote. In this way the religious leaders seek to control the politics and the state-craft. J.D. has already placed great premium on the issue of secularism or communal harmony in its election manifesto (1993).

In case of Bihar, the Muslim common man and state level religious leaders were found to be politically apathetic during 1991 general (Lok Sabha) elections. Those who really matter and who could help provide the masses a direction were so aloof and disinterested that they did not even want to discuss politics, Hazarat Shah Rizwanullah, Sajjadananshin, Khanquah Mujibiah, Phulwarisharif said, "We have no idea of politics, secluded as we are from the public."[34] Ameer-e-shariat for Bihar and Orissa Hazarat Maulana Abdul Rahman disliked to be dragged into any political discussion. Ameer wanted to talk about how Muslims could be uplifted not with the help of political leaders or parties.[35] Some of the Muslim citizens wanted to boycott general elections because parties could not render benefit to them.[36] However, many Muslims wanted to support 'Laloo Yadav's party because he had been successful in curbing communal riots. Noted novelist Abdus Samad opined that Muslims should vote for those forces which fight for their cause at local level.[37] The above statements lead us to the conclusion that Muslims of Bihar want only due share in the polity and betterment of the community in economic and social spheres. They also hate to be called 'Pakistanis'.

The Muslim political leaders from Bihar opposed the call of national Muslim religious leaders breeding fanaticism. All India Muslim Personal Law Board had decided to set up Islamic courts all over India to settle family disputes. But the AICC Minority Cell Chairman (former BPCC Chief) Tarique Anwar described the decision 'improper' and urged the Board to review its decision. He lamented that Muslims were fed up with fundamentalists who have kept them away from national mainstream.[38]

Conclusions

The above discussions underline the following generalisations. The Indian polity is facing minority and majority fanaticism owing to

5. *Ibid.*
6. See D.E. Smith, *India as a Secular State*, New York, Princeton Univ. Press, 1963.
7. Luthera, *op. cit.*, p. 147.
8. 'Jurisdictionalism' implies a state acting in the interest of the entire community to curb the dominance, see Bates, *Religions and Liberty : An Inquiry.*
9. S. Radhakrishnan, *Recovery of Faith.*
10. Luthera, *op. cit.*
11. Constituent Assembly Debates (CAD), Vol. VII, 289.
12. Constituent Assembly Debates (CAD), Vol. VII, 831.
13. H.V. Kamath, CAD, VII, 825-6.
14. M. Ananthasayanam Ayyangar, CAD, VII, 866.
15. See Hoshar Singh, "The Changing Contours of Secularism in India", *Political Science Review*, Vol. 29, Nos. 1-4, Jan.-Dec. 1990, pp. 41-51.
16. The Shah Bano Case, ban on Rushdie's book, repeated use of Abdullah Bukhari for electoral purposes and Congress-Muslim League alliance in Kerala are the burning examples.
17. B.P.R. Vithal, "Roots of Hindu Fundamentalism", *Economic and Political Weekly*, Feb. 20-27, 1993. And also see Krishna Kant, "Religion, Culture, Politics and Nation : Search for a New Equilibrium in Indian Society" *Mainstream*, Annual Number (27 October), 1990.
18. K. Prasad, *op. cit.*
19. Tapan Basu *et al.*, *Khaki Shorts and Saffron Flags*, Orient Longman, 1993.
20. S.R. Maheshwari, "Bill and Checks : Legislation alone cannot wean Religion away from Politics", *The Indian Express*, 20-9-93.
21. T.N. Pandey, "Cynical Partisanship : Delink Corruption from Politics, Not Religion", *The Indian Express*, 20-9-93.
22. Rajeev Dhavan, "Pernicious Bill : The Anti-religion Legislation will Derail the Electoral System", *The Indian Express*, 6-9-93.
23. Ashgar Ali Engineer, "The option : A three-pronged strategy to Decommunalise the Polity", *The Indian Express*, 8-9-93.
24. *The Times of India* (Patna), May 21, 1991, p. 7.
25. V.P. Varma, *Evolution of Politics in Bihar* (Mimeo), Jagjivan Ram Institute of Parliamentary Studies and Political Research (JRIPS), Patna, 1988.
26. V.P. Varma, *A Study of Assembly Elections in Bihar 1967*, I.P.A., Patna University, Patna, 1968.
27. This has been confirmed by Rajani Kothari, "Chunav ke Khel se Nikli Sampradaikta" in Abhya Kumar Dubey (ed.), *Sampradaikta ke shart* (Hindi), Binay Prakashan, Delhi, 1993.

28. See *India Today*, October 15, 1981.

29. The Commission for enquiry of the communal riot in Biharsharif was set up under Bala Subramanium who submitted his report in 1982. For details see "Communal Violence : The Biharsharif", *Economic and Political Weekly*, Feb. 18, 1984.

30. *The Times of India*.

31. *Hindustan Times* (Patna), 18-10-93.

32. Rajani Kothari, *op. cit.*

33. See (i) R.K. Verma and N.P. Yadav, "Caste and Candidate selection : Lok Sabha Poll in Bihar", *Economic & Political Weekly*, June 1-8, 1991, pp. 376-78.

    (ii) R.K. Verma, "Rajnitik Dal, Jati Aur Nirwachan" *Lok Tantra Samiksha*, Vol. 23, Nos. 1-4, Jan.-Dec. 1991, pp. 140-49.

34. Shams Ahmad, "A Community Left Confused by Poll Rhetorics", *The Times of India* (Patna), 14-4-91, p. 1.

35. *Ibid.*

36. *Ibid.*

37. *Ibid.*

38. *The Hindustan Times* (Patna), 13-10-93.

10

INDIAN SECULARISM AND PSEUDO-HINDUISM

Harshvardhan

Secularism, just as C.E.M. Joad's Socialism, is like a hat that has lost its shape because everybody wears it. In the Indian context pseudo-Hindus have made the matter worse by deliberately confusing the masses as well as the intelligentsia. They portray their communal fascism as positive secularism and call genuine secularism pseudo-secularism. To them "fair is foul, and foul is fair". It is a matter of concern that their Goebbelsian propaganda has succeeded to some extent (and mercifully to some extent only) in brainwashing a sizeable section of the society. Against this backdrop it becomes the bounden duty of the secularists to remove the cobwebs of confusion about the concept of Indian secularism which is a bit different from the western one.

To begin with, Indian secularism does *not imply a complete separation of the Church and the State.* This is because, in India there has never been a struggle between the Church (on the organized spiritual power) and the State (on the temporal power). Moreover the western notion has deliberately been disregarded in order to bring about social reforms which often militate against religious customs and rituals. *Sati* system and untouchability are cases in point.

Further, Indian secularism is not *anti-religious*. An anti-religious State, treating religion as the 'Gangotri' of irrationalism, superstitions, error, falsehood, is actively hostile to religion. It restricts religious freedom and discriminates in favour of non-religious. Obviously enough, our secularism does not fall in this category.

If Indian secularism is not anti-religious, it is not *multi-religious* either. A secular state in the sense of multi-religious promotes all religious and discourages atheism. It discriminates against all those who are non-religious. This is not the case with India.

Indian secularism is thus neither separation of the Church and the State nor anti-religious nor multi-religious. It is non-religious and anti-communal. It is marked by an attitude of religious neutrality and equal treatment of all religions and religious minorities. It does not forbid religious or non-religious practices, nor does it show preference for the non-religious over the religious or *vice-versa*. Our Constitution does not discriminate in favour of any religion. In the words of M.C. Setalvad—"The basic idea would seem to be freedom of religion for the individuals, the exclusion by the state of all considerations based on religion in dealing with its citizens and the non-recognition by the state of any particular religion as the state religion."

To Pandit Nehru "It does not mean a state where religion is discouraged. It means freedom of religion and conscience, including freedom for those who have no religion..."

And Mahatma Gandhi translated secularism as "*Sarvadharma Sambhava*." To me, it is the briefest and the best definition of Indian secularism. *Sarvadharma Sambhava* or equal respect for all religions includes respect for even atheism because according to Gandhiji "God is even the atheism of the atheist."

Therefore when Mahatma Gandhi talked of *Ramrajya* it was anything but Hindu Rajya. It was not a theocratic state. Gandhiji categorically stated it a number of times. At one occasion he declared in no uncertain terms, "By Ram Rajya I do not mean Hindu Rajya. I mean by Ram Rajya Divine Rajya—the Kingdom of God. For me Ram and Rahim are one and same deity." In *Harijan* on 18.8.46 he wrote, "when I visit the Frontier Province or address predominantly Muslim audiences I would express my meaning to them by calling it Khadi Raj, while to a Christian audience I would describe it as the Kingdom of God on earth."

Thus while Bapu's Ram Rajya is an epitome of Indian secularism, the Ram Rajya Sangh Parivar is harping on is a symbol of pseudo-Hinduism. It is not Gandhi's Ram Rajya, it is Godse's 'Ram Rajya'.

Today the Mahatma cannot be faulted for the misuse of his secular concept of Ram Rajya by communal leaders because if they are hell-bent on misusing the names of great men, who can stop them. Even the name of Shahid Bhagat Singh was misused by the B.J.P. during the so-called "Ekta Yatra" by Dr. Murli Manohar Joshi. Yes, the name of Bhagat Singh, who was an atheist (not to speak of communal, not even religious), a Marxist (thus to Golwalkar an internal enemy and traitor) and a secularist (in Sangh Parivar's terminology pseudo-secular).

And now witness the prostitution of the name of Vivekanand who always advocated "an Islamic body and a Vedantic head". For Ram's sake please do not misuse the names of the dear departed who cannot come to defend themselves.

Today, the biggest challenge to Indian secularism is from pseudo-Hinduism that is Swadesh-fascism. These pseudo-Hindus have been trying to undermine the secular values of our polity and society by distorting history and popularising communal myths such as minorities are being appeased, Hindus have become second class citizens, Muslims are outsiders and traitors, Hinduism is nationalism, secularism is an alien concept etc.

Now let us examine these myths one by one.

Muslim-appeasement is a hobby horse of the pseudo-Hindus. Actually, appeasement like beauty lies in the eyes of the beholder. It is the selective perception of the pseudo-Hindus that gives them "empirical evidences" of the appeasement of the Muslims. They willy-nilly turn a blind eye to the appeasement of the Hindus and focus their jaundiced eyes on the appeasement of the Muslims. The very idea of Muslim Women's Bill, facilities to Haj Pilgrims, second official language status to Urdu, proposal of opening a Persian University, holidays on Friday in Kerala and the like, is nauseating to them. But these pseudo-Hindus would not pay heed to Somnath Temple renovation by Sardar Patel, unlocking of the Babri Masjid, Shilanyas permission on the disputed site in Ayodhya, the Ramayan and Mahabharat serials on Doordarshan, Hindu rituals like coconut smashing at Govenment. functions Hindu mythological names to military hardware and Government awards, special trains during Hindu festivals, proposal of opening a Vedic University, dropping of Persian and continuation of Sanskrit in the IAS syllabus, conferment of Padma Vibhusan on Atal Bihari Vajpayee, no action against Bal Thackeray despite his bloody role in the Bombay riots and so on.

The selective perception of the saffron-Brigade is also evident from their *communal double standards.* Just contrast the pseudo-Hindus tirade against Muslim Kashmiri militants with their Sphinx-like silence over Hindu ULFA militants of Assam, their campaign against Muslim infiltrators from Bangladesh with inaction against Hindu infiltrators from Nepal and Sri Lanka, their citing triple *Talaq* as an example of pitiable plight of Muslim wives with no comments upon bride burning in the Hindu families, their hue and cry over Shahi Imam's *Fatwa* with their welcome of the V.H.P.'s *Dharm-Sansad's* order..., their *oohing* and *aahing* over infringing of Salman Rushdie's right to expression with their attacking the likes of Nikhil Wagle, ransacking *Sahmat* exhibition, burning Ambedkar's book *"Riddles of Hinduism"*. It is really ironical that the Hindu communalists who have been opposing Muslim Women's Bill are the same people as opposed progressive legislation in favour of the rights of the Hindu women. The Hindutva champions whose hearts bleed for the Muslim women have never opened their mouths against the *"Devadasi"* system which is nothing but pushing Hindu girls into the flesh trade in the name of the Hindu Goddess Yelamma. The pseudo-Hindus who advocate uniform civil code, no doubt a need of the hour, have nothing to say against large scale violation of the age of the consent act on the Akha Teez day in Rajasthan where each year thousands of Hindu children are married off. Pseudo-Hindus should first put their own house in order before picking holes in the Muslims' court. Pot should stop calling the kettle black.

In their hate-campaign against the Muslims, disinformation, misinformation and white lies are also effective weapons in the armoury of pseudo-Hindus. I give you just one example. A relentless communal propaganda by V.H.P.-R.S.S.-B.J.P.-Shivsena combine has led people to believe that within a few years *the Muslims would outnumber the Hindus*, thanks to their being allowed to marry four wives, non-participation in family planning and high fertility rate.

If past censuses are anything to go by the Muslims are not going to be in the majority for hundreds of years to come despite the slightly higher growth rate of Muslim population i.e. 2.7 per cent as against 2.1per cent of annual growth rate of the Hindu population.

Even this higher fertility of Muslims has more to do with their socio-economic backwardness than to their religion. The correlationship between higher fertility rate and Muslim religion must not be misinterpreted as causal-relationship between the two. The dictum "development is the best contraceptive' applies to both Hindus and Muslims.

As regards polygamy, despite the legal permission very few Muslims have more than one wife. Believe it or not, according to the report of the Committee on the Status of Women in India (1975, pp. 66-67) during the decade 1951-61 the percentage of polygamous marriages among Hindus was 5.06 per cent and among Muslims was only 4.31 per cent. Thus polygamy is more prevalent amongst the Hindus than the Muslims, notwithstanding the laws.

Closely related to appeasement-myth is the myth that the *Hindus have been reduced to the second class citizens* and the Muslims are the pampered lot. In this regard I would like to cite some data published by the National Sample Survey Organisation (N.S.S.O.) in 1990 which would explode this myth. Data will speak for themselves. As against only 34.8 per cent of Hindus, 52.3 per cent of Muslims live below the poverty line; as against 33.4 per cent of illiterate Hindus there are 50.5 per cent of Muslims who are not literate, as against 21 per 1,000 Hindu households there are only 7 per 1,000 Muslim households that possess more than 8 hectares of land, as against 467 per 1,000 Hindu salaried households there are only 289 per 1,000 Muslim salaried households. Needless to say the list is not exhausted.

	Hindus	Muslims
Below poverty line (%)	34.8	52.3
Illiterate (%)	33.4	50.5
Land possession (above 8 hectares)	21 per 1,000	7 per 1,000
Regular/Wage salaried	467 per 1,000	289 per 1,000

Yet another anti-secular stance of pseudo-Hindus is their *equating Hinduism with nationalism.* This is not only anti-secular but also based on falsehood. The experiences of Pakistan show that religion cannot be the basis of nationalism. The birth of Bangladesh as well as the problems in Sind, Baluchistan and the NWFP are conclusive examples of the fact. Fascist parties more often than not put on the mark of nationalism. Whether it was Nazi (National Socialist), Lepen's National Front of France, new-born British National Party (BNP) or the Rashtriya Swayam Sevak Sangh (R.S.S.) in India. Please note the word 'National' or 'Rashtriya' in all these fascist organisations. Pandit Nehru in an article published in *The Tribune* long back in November 1933 rightly commented—"It must be remembered that communalism of a majority community must of necessity bear a closer resemblance to nationalism than the communalism of a minority group."

Patriotism or nationalism is not the monopoly of the Hindus. For the Sangh Parivar an affluent Hindu NRI feathering his nest in the USA, Canada or Britain is a greater patriot than a Muslim weaver in Andhra Pradesh or a Christian fisherman in Kerala contributing their bit to the Indian economy. Nationalism is a secular concept, it must not be communalized.

It must not be forgotten that whenever or wherever in the name of nationalism the majority community has tried to impose its will over the minority community by force, the result is *civil war, chaos and even disintegration* of the country. S.W.R.D. Bhandaranaike's "Sinhala only" slogan and anti-minority (Tamil) policies have led to Tamil terrorism and unending civil war in Sri Lanka. In retrospect his "Sinhala only" policy has not even benefited the majority Sinhala community. Mandir-warriors should take a lesson or two from the Sri Lankan experiences. Similarly, Milosevic's Serbian Chauvinism, like L.K. Advani's Hindutva, has led to civil war and disintegration of Yugoslavia which had remained a unified and prosperous country under Marshall Tito's Nehruvian rule. History is replete with such examples. If we fail to understand the fact that secularism is not only necessary for minorities only but also for the very survival and existence of our beloved India, then perhaps it would be too late. In Md. Iqbal's words *"Na Samjhoge To Mit Jaoge Ee Hind Ke Logon, Tumhari Dastan Bhi Na Rahegi Dastano Mein"* (O people of India if you don't understand you will be eliminated, even your story will not find a place in history).

Just as nationalism is not Hinduism, Indian culture is not Hindu culture. Ours is a composite culture. To each and every sphere of our culture, be it dance, drama, painting, sculpture, architecture, literature, language, costumes etc., the non-Hindu contributions are invaluable which we cannot wish away. The culture the pseudo-Hindus stand for is not our glorious culture but vulture-culture.

The Sangh Parivar is a *multi-headed monster* whose different heads speak different languages with an eye to different target groups. Anti-Muslim vulgar slogans are made popular by the rank and file of the so-called Parivar (Ganga would be a better word) with the consent of their leaders. The leaders would in turn couch the same sentiments in high sounding words like "cultural nationalism, Hindu identity, *Sanskar* and *Sanskriti*, *Bhakti* combined with *Shakti* and so on to fool the intelligentsia. Mahanths and Sadhus would cite scriptures like Shakespearean devils to woo and God-fearing religious people and the likes of Swapan Dasgupta and Arun Shourie would take care of westernised sections of the society.

Mind you, pseudo-Hinduism is not only anti-Muslim, anti-secular, anti-national but also anti-Hindu. Ram has been converted into Rambo, Hindus into barbarians wanting an eye for an eye, a tooth for a tooth. Mandir into a means to become Mantri and festivals into occasions to whip up Hindu hysteria. In short pseudo-Hinduism in the name of *Sanskriti* (culture) is reviving all superstitions, outdated rituals, inhuman rites and inegalitarian and stratified social system. Thus, reason which is a basic ingredient of secularism is the first casualty of *Hindu revivalism*. Glorification of *Sati* system in the wake of Roop Kunwar's butchery at Deorala by Vijya Raje Sindhia incidentally a widow, Vamdev's justification of caste system and opposition to protective discrimination, deafening silence by Hindutva leaders over Harijan-Hunting and their persecution over temple and tree issue and the present preparation for *Aswamedha Yagya* here at Patna are some examples of their medieval outlook. In a Hindu Rashtra Dr. Ambedkar's secular constitution would be replaced by Manusmriti in which for instance slaying women, *shudra* is described as minor offences (Manusmriti XI, 67). Therefore, Shambukes and Sitas, beware of Hindu Rashtra.

The votaries of pseudo-Hinduism claim that *Muslims are outsiders and invaders* and it is the Hindus and Hindus alone who are the original inhabitants of India. Nothing can be farther from truth. One need not become a historian to know that even the Aryans had come from outside as invaders on horseback. Lokamanya Tilak perhaps a greater authority on the issue than Uma Bharti and Ritambhara, considered Arctic Zone as the original home of the Aryans. The R.S.S. Guru Golwalkar while accepting Tilak's thesis asserted that Arctic Zone was originally that part of the globe which is today known as Bihar and Orissa. The Arctic Zone, Guruji claims in his favourite book "We or our nationhood defined", gradually moved to its present position. In this context Mr. Sitaram Yechury rightly points out "even by the logic of his own argument if the Arctic Zone moved away from Bihar-Orissa, how could it leave behind the people who were inhabiting that land mass? When the land mass moves, it moves along with everything on it. People cannot be left hanging in a vacuum only to drop down when and where Golwalkar wishes. This is Golwalkar's "Golmal" logic.

It is interesting to note that the *"thekedars"* of Hindu Dharma not only call Muslims alien but also the very concept of secularism alien. Pseudo-Hindus who are all praise for an alien Adolf Hitler, Guru of Guru Golwalkar, call *secularism an alien concept* forgetting King Ashoka's Dhamma, emperor Akbar's *Din-Ilahi* and *Sulh-E-Kul*, *Sufi* and *Bhakti* movements and to crown it all the essentially secular character of Indian culture and tradition. Even today the Indian masses are more religious than communal, and our hope lies there.

The pseudo-Hindus are out to make the religious communal. By playing upon the religious sentiments of the Hindu masses and widening the Hindu-Muslim divide they have succeeded in reaping a rich electoral harvest. They have made Ram a pawn on the chess-board of politics. The Lotus symbol on the Toyota Rath of L.K. Advani, during his riot *Yatra* from Somnath to Ayodhya (or Samastipur), is quite revealing. *Mandir Ke Piche Kya Hai* we must not forget. It is not devotion to Ram but lust for power. Why did not L.K. Advani and Atal Bihari Vajpayee, who are cast in the mould of Adolf Hitler, utter a single word about the Babri Masjid while they were the cabinet ministers in Mr. Morarji Desai's Ministry? Actually at that time they were already in power. Moreover, the same leaders as are criticising Muslim vote bank politics are indulging in Hindu vote bank robbery. The anti-Muslim, anti-Hindu, anti-national and anti-secular pseudo-Hindus must be exposed.

Secularism has to be spread as an active and vibrant ideology throughout the country. Bipan Chandra rightly argues that the way out of communalism implies a strategy of decommunalising the masses. At the ideological plane pseudo-Hinduism has to be defeated. If the B.J.P. and its gangs are repeating lies hundreds of times with the hope that they will stick at last once, we secularists should also repeat the truth as long as there is even one person who refuses to believe it. Hopefully, in this hegemonic struggle for the minds and the hearts of the people truth alone will prevail (*Satyameva Jayate*).

11

SECULARISM AND INDIAN FORMAL EDUCATION

R.P. Sinha

I

One of the paradoxical and vexing dilemmas of India's national development has been its continuous experimentation with the programmes and contents of formal education. During pre- as well as post-independence periods, various committees and advisory boards were, and continue to be even today, set up to advise and direct the government to contemplate and devise ways and means to accomplish the task of providing secular education and equality of educational opportunities to its citizens.[1] The need to spread education has been heightened by the consciousness of the role education plays in the development process of a society. This role is manifest in at least three major respects : *First*, the very historical transformation of the country from colonial status to a free nation, usually believed to be a product of educated minorities of the western secular variety, has led to positive relationship between formal education and formation of elite. Formal education as a consequence has become one of the most sought-after goals among the citizens; *Second*, it is widely recognised that formal, secular education is an indispensable prerequisite for economic growth and social modernization. It has been simultaneously recognized that economic growth is indispensable for the creation of minimal conditions for meaningful national development and well-being; *Third*, formal-secular education has increasingly acquired importance in the development process because it is believed that without expansion of secular education, India cannot enter into technological stage and become modern, a premise very closely attuned to the prerequisites of modernisation of a society.[2] In addition to insatiable demands for technological advancement and economic growth, enormous pressures for the expansion of secular education are also mounted by the imperatives of equality, social justice, secularism *et al.* It is in nutshell believed that education is a prime requisite for national preparedness for development.

Notwithstanding concerted attempts to achieve egalitarian education through amorphous human resources and colossal investments, the system of formal education has not been able to deliver the results. The professed creation of egalitarian society through formal-secular education has remained unfulfilled at least on two counts : *First*, the system of institutionalized *formal education has unmistakably followed* the colonial legacy whereby heterogeneity has increased manifold with obvious repercussions on social groups; and *second*, despite avowed promises, formal education has increased the chasm of discrimination and disparities between the classes[3] and also between communities on communal lines. These are manifest in several respects. *First*, the contents of education are overwhelmingly in dissonance with stark realities of social milieu. As a result the curricula and textbooks reflect "the values and visions of colonial bureaucracy"[4] which are divisive in content. *Second*, the implications of education in terms of development of an egalitarian secular society need reexamination. It is feared particularly in respect of higher education that "the very process of education instead of creating a sense of justice, equality and rationalism has been responsible for inculcating differentiation"[5] evidences of which are clearly discernible today in the form of sectarian institutions, minority schools and colleges and the like, thus leading to the creation of, and encouragement to, divisive, non-secular and sectarian forces in the society, in general, and in the academia and educational institutions, in particular. As a result the system of formal education in India has been, by and large, unresponsive and blunted to the demands of a secular society.

II

The bone of contention therefore is : Is India's formal education secular in content and form? Can it be secular in content and form in present day India? The basic premise to be contested and examined is : is the Indian formal education non-secular, and sectarian? In order to examine this it is imperative to delve deep into the process of development of formal education in India.

Educational institutions during the early period of British paramountcy in India functioned as an instrument of intellectual, cultural and political socialization and in the process it attempted to instil in them cultural values specific to the aliens. The function of formal education was apparently designed to provide the British power with "a class of clerks, bureaucrats and political collaborators."[6] Instrumentality of these functions was inexorably intertwined; *first*, as an agent for modernizing intellectual-cultural activity and, *second*, as an instrument of British cultural and political domination and hegemony. Until 1828, the British tended to prize Indian learning, tried to rationalize and modernize it and to introduce modern scientific ideas within its framework. Indians too looked forward to taking account of European knowledge. But this complementarity ended soon with the advent of MacCaulay, who denounced and abhorred the continuance of Indian system of knowledge and education and proclaimed that "a single shelf of a good European library was worth the whole native literature of India and Arabia".[7] His contemptuous denouncement, which vividly reflected the changed tenor of the British policy on India, marked the beginning of decadence and introduction of an educational policy that replaced the Indian native system with English learning. The resources were now placed at the disposal of English language educational institutions, thus leaving the Indian native education sagging for want of encouragement. The changed policy adopted by the British through MacCaulay symbolized the rise of radical asymmetry in British-Indian cultural relation and made copying the dominator a compulsory condition of higher education.[8]

Gradually, mastery of cultural elements of English education, a good command of the language and literature and English manners became the qualifying conditions for access to opportunities in the public services and private firms. English education thus introduced yet another civilizational element into the multi-civilizational syncretism that is Indian culture.[9] Thus knowledge was what the new education was to give but its inner agenda was to improve conduct based on English education. Education in this context of learning became less important than the moral influence it was supposed to exercise.[10] But moral influence was euphemism for Christian ethics. British education thus: (a) influenced the self-perception of the educated Indians; (b) helped them achieve new status in the society vis-a-vis illiterate ones; (c) helped create a new class which was starkly different from the native ones—a peculiar amalgamation of Indo-European features; (d) helped emerge a new sense of loyalty and dignity—the educated man's loyalty to the Empire was distinct from others as it had added components of faith in oneself as a product of education;[11] (e) encouraged entrepreneurship in education through its grants-in-aid allurement which subserved latent intentions of politicizing educational institutions. Thus the educational objectives of the early schools and colleges that thrived under the grants-in-aid policy were cultural and characterological.[12] The British Raj was engaged in making concerted efforts to produce Christian virtues and was fervently impassioned to transfer English culture and learning. With this objective in view, the interference of the government escalated and now it determined the educational goals and resources of these institutions to subserve partisan, self-interest and ideological ends of the British in India. Thus there was sufficient scope and mechanism to propagate sectarian ideology and principle. It conveniently led to proselytisation of the illiterate, lower class, lower caste Hindus and Muslims who constituted the overwhelming section of India's population.

III

The reaction of Reform and Independence movements in India to British paramountcy and particularly to proselytisation was spontaneous and vociferous. The accent of the British on privatisation of educational institutions provided fresh impetus to renaissance and freedom leaders to do the same and paved the way for them to launch socio-political reform movements through educational institutions. These leaders in doing so manifestly aimed at restoration of Indian (Hindu) culture and value and latently fuelled anti-secular forces although their intention was to seize the spread of Christianity in India. The increasing interest in awareness of founding educational institutions led to private entrepreneurship in the arena of formal education which gradually became responsible for the founding of a large number of schools and colleges. Such private entrepreneurship could be identified as nationalist and sectarian movement.[13] Over and above, the expansion of educational institutions witnessed the entry of philanthropists in the field of education, who too founded several educational institutions. Stalwarts like Balgangadhar Tilak and Gopal Krishna Gokhale were the notable ones who formed the Deccan Educational Society.[14] These attempts championed the cause of nationalist movement, were antagonistic to the process of proselytisation and were in essence antagonistic to the English pattern of education. These attempts and other such movements that followed were essentially anti-secular, pro-Hindu in character as they waged a war against Christianity and encouraged the converted Christians to go back into the fold of Hinduism again; and they did it primarily through educational institutions.

The other two types of private entrepreneurship, the one based on sect and the other on caste communities, were in fact inalienable parts of cultural reform and 'group-solidarity'[15] movements of the nineteenth and twentieth centuries. The Hindus as well as the Muslims and also the Sikhs through their *Khalsa* movement responded to one another and to the western and Christian impact by founding educational institutions that propagated their cultural moorings and identity. Several caste communities too vided with each other to forge ahead and come to the forefront. They followed the footsteps of the nationalist movement to maintain their group solidarity and preserve and/or augment their social status. They found it apt to found educational institutions. In the process "several castes, e.g. *Vaishyas*, *Kayasthas*, *Rajputs*, *Nairs*, *Bhumihars* in particular, founded their institutions,"[16] to sustain and improve their high status. This could be largely done by facilitating access to modern educational opportunities. The forging of communities in the domain of education and their perceived advantages of education as an instrument of movement in the vertical social order fascinated other caste-communities. The lower ones, "the *Jats, Ahirs, Ezhavas, Nadars, Mahars and Lingayats,*"[17] followed the higher castes which was a sufficient testimony to the willingness and capacity of these castes—the untouchables—for self-mobilization and organisation.

In pursuit of reform and nationalist activities, several organizations were set up and quite a few of them were involved in the expansion of education to subserve the latent functions i.e., spread of Hinduism. The educational activities of Arya Samaj, for example, which was a staunch Hindu reform organisation, send us clear indications as to how the protagonists of reform movement, within the rubric of Hinduism, made education and educational institutions a tool of expressing cultural norms and identity as well as restoration and preservation of Hinduism. The Arya Samaj championed the cause of Hinduism, stood erect to withstand the onslaughts and proselytisation and made concerted efforts to strengthen Hinduism against its Christian and Muslim competitors by emphasizing the unity of Hinduism found in Vedic literature. The apparent manifestations of these efforts were vividly displayed in the opening of *Gurukulas*, patterned on the ancient educational institutions. The *Gurukulas* laid great emphasis on the study of ancient Hindu texts and literature. The educational institutions of the *Samaj* were christened *Dayanand Anglo-Vedic* (DAV) Colleges/ Schools.

The Arya Samaj faced serious challenges from Sanatana Dharma Sabha (SDS) which was founded in 1895 in Delhi. The Sanatana movement created a substantial number of educational institutions, though the protagonists of the movement had latent intention of protecting *Hinduism* against the religious reform movement conceived and enunciated by Arya Samaj and Brahmo Samaj. However, the Sanatana found the Samaj a protector of Hinduism and gradually grew closer to Samaj. Both of them had gradually grown conservative, were protagonists of religious fundamentalism and both were opposed to secularism and Islam.[18] The inner desire of the Sabha and Arya Samaj of founding Hindu educational institutions was almost coincidental with the Muslim efforts who too were busy in doing the same. As a consequence several institutions of formal education were also set up by the Muslim community.[19] Among the most prominent institutions to emerge from the reform movements of the 19th century include Mohammadan Anglo Oriental College which was later destined to adorn the name of Aligarh Muslim University. The Oriental College was not the solitary example of outgrowth of the efforts of the Muslim community. Delhi College, which was founded in 1824, grew out of Madarsah Ghaziyuddin.[20] And it was soon followed by a number of institutions of education which were founded particularly as a precursor to Dar-ul-Ulum, a movement to spread and champion Muslim orthodoxy and fundamentalism which vigorously resisted and opposed English and Western culture and Hindu fundamentalism and in doing so it castigated Hindu revivalism and culture.[21] Christian Colleges, on the other hand, which had the benefit of support from the imperial presence, reflected in no uncertain measure the tendency of social and religious movements to express themselves in educational terms.

A micro-aggregative picture thus tends to reflect formation of number of educational institutions which were set up by sectarian and religious bodies. These organisations tried tooth and nail to insulate 'own' society from the spread of 'other' fundamentalism and vied with each other to encapsulate 'own communities' from the influences of other fundamental tendencies and accompanying forces. Institutions of formal education during nationalist movement were thus primarily the carriers of preserving and sustaining identity of individual communities and thus were effective insulators and encapsulators.

IV

The role of institutions of formal education on the eve of Indian independence was replication of what it was during the earlier periods. Various Commissions were set up to examine formal education and the role of religious fundamentalism and to look into the desirability and viability of introducing religious education in the curricula and syllabi of formal education. The first among such Commissions was the *University Education Commission* (1948-49)[22] which was constituted by the Government of India. Popularly known as Radhakrishnan Commission, a leading scholar of religion,[23] this Commission dealt extensively with education in context of religion and secularism. The underlying arguments of the Commission's recommendations were: (a) dogmatic religion leads to conflict; (b) religious conflict leads to secular state; (c) the secular state bans only dogmatic religious instructions; and (d) the state can and should provide for teaching of universal religion.[24] It is significant to note that the Commission recommended the need of introducing teaching of universal religion. Among other recommendations, the Commission exhorted that students should study the lives of religious leaders.

Another significant attempt at the direction of whether or not educational institutions should incorporate inputs of religion in the course-content was made by the *Constitution of India*, through the sections viz., 15(1), 28(1), 28(2), 28(3) etc. These provisions stipulated for: (1) institutions maintained by the government; (2) state-recognized institutions; (3) state-aided institutions; (4) institutions established under any endowment but administered by the government. It is stipulated that educational institutions, falling under the categories of 1, 2 and 3, cannot provide for religious education, that is, the contents and syllabi of educational instruction shall not incorporate inputs of religion and that these institutions shall not impart instructions in religious education and would be thus secular in character. In case of institutions falling under the category 4, that is, institutions established under any endowment or trust and are administered by the state, 'there is no restriction on such instructions.[25] Implicit in this freedom is the freedom to impart religious instructions by institutions of formal education (by minority, non-Hindu Communities) and that the State will not intervene in its affairs to the extent that these institutions follow a particular religious syllabus of instruction. Put in another way, the State will safeguard their interest in matters of curriculum, syllabus and medium of instruction. It obviously leads to the premise that India has accepted the principle of secularism in educational matters with the imprint of constitutional sanctions. This principle does not imply so much as separation between state and religion as a state's involvement in religion, provided it is non-discriminate between different religions.'[26]

Another official committee set up to look into the problem of secular education was *Secondary Education Commission* (1952-53)[27] which suggested that 'if at all such instructions could be done, it must be privately organized.'[28] It recommended that 'religious instructions *may be given* in schools only on voluntary basis and outside the regular school hours. Such instructions being confined to the children of particular faith concerned and given with the consent of the parents and the management.[29] The Commission further recommended that 'no book prescribed as a text book...contain any passage or statement...offend the religious or social susceptibilities of any section of the community or might indoctrinate the minds of the young students with particular political or religious ideologies.'[30]

Another Committee on Religious and Moral Instruction[31] was set up in 1959 to make a detailed study of the entire problem of religious and moral education in educational institutions. The Committee made different recommendations for different stage, of education. Thus for elementary stage, the Committee advocated for holding school assembly and group singing, inclusion of lives and teachings of prophets, saints and religious leaders and setting aside a period or two every week for moral instruction. The Committee thought it prudent to make other recommendations like inviting speakers to address the students on moral and spiritual values. It also recommended for convening joint celebrations on the occasion of important festivals of all religions. For the University students, the Committee recommended to adopt the recommendations of University Education Commission.

Committee on Emotional Integration (1961-62)[32] was set up to examine the question of the role of religion in emotional integration. It concluded that although it is not possible to provide religious education as a part of curriculum for schools in a secular state, education will be incomplete if students are not helped to appreciate the spiritual values which the various religions present to the people. The *Education Commission* (1964-66)[33] noted that the recommendations of neither the UEC (1948) nor the CRMI (1959) had made any appreciable impact. The Commission recommended in favour of religious instructions and it said "...syllabus giving well-chosen information about each of the major religions should be included...it should highlight fundamental similarities in the great religions...have a common course on this subject in all parts of the country and common text books which should be prepared at the national level...worthwhile to have them scrutinized by a small Committee...to ensure that nothing is included in them to which any religious group could take legitimate objections."[34]

V

The preceding discussion leads to several mind-boggling issues. In the Indian context, formal education during the British and post-British era has subserved—*first*, as an agent of proselytisation whereby the natives were converted into Christians which helped create a band of dedicated Indians who had imbibed alien culture to serve the imperial officialdom in India; *second*, the system of formal education provided scope and means for the restoration of Indian culture and value which was vehemently spearheaded by different reform movements. It was basically a reaction to British policy of proselytisation and was Hindu in character and form, enunciated by staunch protagonists of Hinduism, e.g., Arya Samaj, Prarthana Samaj, Sanatana Dharma, Brahmo Samaj and the like. These organisations through their movements tried to insulate the local communities against conversion. But at the same time these movements provided and encouraged apertures by which the natives could, through the means of formal education, learn and accept the finer elements of European scientific knowledge and technological development. Thus while these reformists created insulators through reform movements against proselytisation, they encouraged apertures for the acceptance of European knowledge of science and technology among the Indians; *third*, in the process, the Muslims tried to forge ahead to overcome the problem of identity crisis. The acknowledged problem cropped up due to the British policy of proselytisation on the one hand and Indians' (Hindus') reaction to restoration of Hinduism on the other. As a result the protagonists of Islam advocated for incorporating religious instructions, based on the tenets of *Quran*, and launched struggles for its inclusion in the curriculum of formal education; *fourth*, due to persistent attempts at conversion, the British Government feared difficulties and were apprehensive of defiance from the native communities. As a consequence, it favoured the notion of religious neutrality and consequently kept the government institutions of formal education beyond the purview of religious instructions in formal education. But it nevertheless permitted the government-aided, privately-managed educational institutions to impart religious instructions beyond the normal working hours, and granted complete freedom to unaided, private educational institutions to follow their own syllabi. Thus for the British, the question of religious neutrality was the manifest agenda in formal education, religious instructions in education was its latent intention; *fifth*, during the post-British period, particularly the first few decades after the Independence, formal education was the replication of the older edifice and it has remained almost unaltered, save minor tinkerings, even today. Several reports, numerous commissions and innumerable workshops on formal education (e.g., U.E.C. 1948-49, S.E.C. 1952-53) clearly bring out these astounding facts. Even the Indian Constitution has made recommendations in favour of religious neutrality on the one hand and has permitted the state-aided and unaided private institutions of formal education to impart instructions on religious education, on the other.

VI

A perusal of the pattern of development of formal education in the context of secularism in India raises a number of questions and each question tends to indicate dilemmas that the Indian government encounters in respect of formal education. The *foremost* question that torments the minds of intellectuals and policy-makers alike is—should religious instructions in formal education be imparted at all? It tends to point to an ambivalent situation, i.e., if formal education is allowed to incorporate elements of religion, will it be secular and as a consequence, all-encompassing? This dilemma refers to the choice between *Affectivity and Affective-Neutrality*. This question leads to three distinct choices: (a) should it be religion-free formal education, i.e., no education in any religious instructions is imparted; (b) should it be mono-religious education, i.e., formal education would incorporate in its ambit dissemination of instructions in one, may be locally dominant, religion, and (c) should it be multi-religious in which the syllabi of formal education would incorporate elements of different religions with an accent on morality and virtues of each religion?

The *second* concomitant and inalienable dilemma which arrests our immediate attention is : what types of educational institutions would impart, if at all, education in religious instructions? This dilemma refers to the choice between *Universalism and Particularism*. That is, should all institutions or should a select few (minority ones) impart education in religious instructions? This posits that should all educational institutions, irrespective of their being government-run or privately-managed, impart religious education or should it be confined to *some* (private ones) with or without grant-in-aid status. The third option is : *no* educational institution should impart courses on religious instruction. This dilemma refers to a vexing situation. An examination would indicate two succinct but critical areas of educational policy of the government: (a) educational policy of the government in relation to government-run educational institutions, and (b) educational policy of the government in relation to government-aided or unaided institutions of formal education.[35]

The *third* dilemma is concerned with the selection, management and administration of institutions of formal education and the role of the government. Several reports on minority educational institutions, institutions of formal education under private enterprises, indicate little or no role of the government. Should selection of teachers, admission of students and management of the schools be based on merit and performance or should the government sanction funds and grants-in-aid on the basis of declared quality of the educational institutions? This dilemma refers to the choice between *Quality* and *Performance*. The dilemma offers at least three possible options: (a) Should admission of students, recruitment of teachers, representatives to Board of Management and grant-in-aid to institutions of formal education be open to all sections of the society, based on merit, qualification and achievement? (b) Should these be confined to a *particular* segment of society, based mainly on considerations other than merit and qualifications? The third option is that *all* institutions of formal education are treated equally in terms of admission of students, recruitment of teachers, administration of institutions and grant-in-aid and the government should evolve a uniform policy.

The *fourth* dilemma is concerned with the aims of the nation that it has set forth to promote and accomplish through the system of formal education. This refers to the choice between *Insulators and Apertures,* i.e., the nation allowing religion-based development or the nation allowing access to modern scientific knowledge. It reflects in essence whether the nation formulates development plans keeping in view the religious values and encourages the same through the institutions of formal education, thus insulating its society from permeating influences of other religion or whether the developmental goals are set out and implemented in utter disregard to religious priorities.

In view of the growing technological and scientific advancement in India in particular and the world in general, and also in view of the much orchestrated proclamations of creating a socially just, democratic, progressive society, the major dilemma before the Indian planners is—are these ends better promoted by having no education in religious instruction in any institution of formal education.

VII

These dilemmas which the Indian government encounters require deep probing and these cannot be answered without reference to the goals the Indian nation has set for itself. It is generally agreed that India, in its voyage to development and modernization, has set out to be a modern, socially just, democratic, equalitarian and economically progressive nation. This is clearly discernible in its various programmes and its declared constitutional obligations. The protagonists of secularism hold that the system of formal education should be entirely secular as the study of religious instructions in educational institutions will lead to the emergence and perpetuation of regressive, sectarian and undemocratic forces. These protagonists have several instances to offer to buttress their contention. For example S.A. Khundmiri has provided in an appendix to a Textbook on Indian History for third standard students of Andhra Pradesh several examples which eulogise the Hindu kings and refer the Muslims with contempt.[36] Almost all history books, prescribed for different courses, are replete with such accounts. It is mentioned umpteen times that the Muslims invaded India; that they destroyed Hindu shrines; that they forcibly married Hindu women; that Muslim rulers had innumerable Hindu women in their *Harems,* etc. Notwithstanding these historical realities, veracity of which is historically established, description of such accounts in text books is sufficient to antagonise young minds, fuel anti-Muslim feelings among them and shape their tender minds accordingly. The non-secular and sectarian descriptions in text books are further accentuated by nostalgic descriptions which hold Hindu Rajas in high esteem vis-a-vis Muslim rulers. Descriptions* in Text Book on History in Hindi run like this : *"Akbar ek mahan shashak tha ... Shivaji ek yoddha the ... Maharana Pratap veergati ko prapta huye ... Humayun mar gaya ..."* Such descriptions using uncomplimentary language for the Muslims (e.g. *tha, gaya*) and eulogisation for the Hindus (e.g. *the*, *huye*) are sufficient to influence the sensitive minds and critical faculties of the students.

Analogous is the situation with administration and management of institutions of formal education. Many educational institutions with designated minority status have introduced their own systems of management. These institutions have made compulsory for students the chanting of *mantras*, supplication at *havans*, recitation of *ayaats*

* These descriptions have been taken from Text Book on History in Hindi prescribed by Bihar Text Book Committee for the students of Seventh Standard.

of *Quran* and *stanzas* from *Bible.* These practices do not encourage students of different faiths to block together and seek admission in such institutions. In many minority institutions, knowledge of Urdu has been made obligatory for the appointment of Hindi teachers in Urdu schools. These and similar practices give rise to fissiparous and divisive tendencies, insulate the academics from modern, non-secular influences and consequently generate among sections of society a feeling of alienation. Such recordings of India's history and practices described above tend to "offer bases for questioning the Indian state as a secular national identity". [37]

All this poses serious problems and has obvious implications for what history will be taught through the system of formal education and what kind of civil society, in which the young ones are expected to live the rest of their lives, is visualized.[38]

Nevertheless, it may be argued, and not erroneously, that the Indian society presents the existence of different religions having separate histories and representing different and diverse attitudes towards life and morality. Seen in this context, social obligations offer a great challenge to the spirit of secularism. Since adherence to one or many religious instructions in institutions of formal education will tend to lead to divisive and sectarian tendencies and since special status to educational institutions will tend to precipitate these further, it may be argued that it is scientific education which should be made compulsory. The protagonists of this view (e.g. Sinha, 1968) contend that complete separation of education from religion seems to be the first step. Rather than promotion of religious education, the evolution of secular, scientific education seems to be important. "The structure of the educational system, operating in conjunction with diverse social processes, tends to produce a broad unifying tendency..." (Shukla, 1992, 209) and therefore it is secular and scientific education in institutions of formal education which would seize and encapsulate the growth of divisive, sectarian and non-secular tendencies.

REFERENCES

1. Jha, B.K. (1984) : Growth of Education and Political Development in India, in Prasad, B. and Singh, S.P. (eds.), Aspects of Education and Politics in India, Swarna, Patna.

2. Several scholars working in this area have highlighted this issue. See for example Lerner, D., Passing of Traditional Society, Macmillan, London, 1964; Dube, S.C., 'Modernization and Its Adaptive Demands in Papers in Sociology of Education is India, N.C.E.R.T., Delhi, 1967; Dube S.C., Modernization and Development; Alternative Paradigm, Vistaar, Delhi, 1998; Singh, Yogendra, Modernization of Indian Tradition, Rawat, Jaipur, 1986.

3. See for example Sinha, R.P. 'Equality of Educational Opportunities in the context of Development', ICAES Symposium, World Cong. of Anthrop., Yugoslavia, 1988; Sinha, R.P. (ed.), "General Introduction", Dimensions of Indian Education, Har Annand, Delhi, 1994.

4. Kumar, Krishna (1991): Political Agenda of Education: A Study in Colonialist and Capitalist Ideas, Sage, Delhi.

5. Singh, N.K. (1979): Education and Social Change, Rawat, Jaipur.

6. Rudolph, S.H. and Rudolph, L.I. (1972): Education and Politics in India, Oxford, Delhi.

7. *Rudolph and Rudolph, op. cit.*

8. *ibid.*

9. *ibid.*

10. Walsh, J.E. (1983): Growing up in British India, Holmes Mier, New York.

11. Krishna Kumar, *op. cit.*

12. Rudolph and Rudolph, *op. cit.*

13. See Nurullah, S. and Naik, J.P. A History of Education in India, MacMillan, Bombay, 1943; Wilkinson, R. (ed.), Gentlemanly Bower, Oxford University Press, Oxford, 1966.

14. Rudolph, S.H. and Rudolph, L.I. (1967) : The Modernity of Indian Tradition, Chicago University Press, Chicago.

15. Krishna Kumar, *op. cit.*

16. Rudolph and Rudolph, *op. cit.*

17. Rudolph and Rudolph, 1967, *op. cit.*

18. See for example Hiemsath, C. Indian Nationalism and Hindu Social Reform, Princeton University Press, Princeton, 1964; Rudolph and Rudolph, 1972, *op. cit.*

19. The Khaksar movement, the funding of Madarasas, the dissemination of Knowledge of Koran at masjids were some examples. For details, see Smith, W.C., Modern, Islam in India, Usha, Delhi, 1979.

20. Mujeej, M. (1967) : The Indian Muslim, London.

21. Faruqi, Zeya-UT (1963) : The Devband School and the Demand of Pakistan, Bombay.

22. University Education Commission (1948-49) : Govt. of India.

23. Mahadevan, TMP (1971) : Outlines of Hinduism, Chetana, Bombay.

24. Smith, D.E. (1963) : India as a Secular State, Princeton Univ. Press, Princeton.

25. Bhatt, B.D. and J.C. Aggarwal (eds.) (1969); Educational Documents in India (1813-1968), Arya Book Depot, Delhi.

26. Sinha, V.K. (ed.) (1968) : Secularism in India, Balvani, Bombay.

27. Secondary Education Commission (1954) Report of the Commission, Min. of Education, G.O.I.

28. Sinha, 1967, *op. cit.*

29. Biswas, A and S. Agrawal (eds.) (1971) : Indian Educational Documents Since Independence, The Academic Publishers, New Delhi.

30. Biswas and Agrawal, *op. cit.*

31. Committee on Religious and Moral Instruction (1960), Report of the Committee, Min. of Education, G.O.I.

32. Committee on Emotional Integration (1962) Report, Min. of Education, Govt. of India.

33. Education Commission (1966) Report of the Commission (1964-66) Min. of Education, G.O.I.

34. See Education Commission Report, *op. cit.*

35. Sharma, Arvind (1987) : 'Religious Traditions in Modern Indian Educational Policy and Practice' in Ghosh, R. and Zacharia M. (eds.), Education and the Process of Changes, Sage, Delhi.

36. See Sinha, 1967, *op. cit.*; Sharma, *op. cit.*

37. Shukla, Suresh (1992) : Pluralism and Education in India : Problems and Prospects; *Prospects*, Vol. XXII, No. 2 (82), UNESCO.

38. See Shukla, *op. cit.*

12

FUNDAMENTALIST RELIGIOUS REVIVAL : IMPACT ON THE DALITS

A.K. Lal

Fundamentalism implies faithful adherence to a core of ideas and actions laid down in the sacred texts. It seeks a return to the 'pure standards' of the ancient times. It represents "an outlook based on extreme conservatism in matters of religion or other traditional belief systems" (Talib 1993: 37). Fundamentalism accords respect to orthodoxy and "seeks a greater extra-ecclesiastical role and voice for the clergy. It is much more than a religious revivalism" (Khare 1986:14).

India today stands "on the threshold of some sort of native fascism" (Gould 1993). *Hindutva* represents a palpable resurgent, united and increasingly militant movement of Hindu revivalism. Saffron is no longer a colour of renunciation but that of reassertion. *Hindutva* projects an image of tumultuous violence. The militancy of the organised Hindu backlash has dragged the country into a communal cauldron. The pathfinders of *Hindutva* have aroused and manipulated the religious sentiments, ensuring in their wake a blood-bath across the country. The majority appears to have developed a minority psyche. "*Hindutva* is a political ideology shaped by Hindu fundamentalists out of the 'little' or 'folk' tradition of Hinduism with its colourful and noisy emphasis on temples and idol worship" (Talib 1993: 38). This fundamentalism is characterised by sudden and unprecedented assertiveness of militant Hinduism. It is threatening to the secular fabric of Indian society as it prefers conflict to accommodation.

Hindutva at this moment is in a triumphant mood having emerged ideologically as a viable alternative to the Gandhi-Nehru legacy of a democratic State, professing adherence to social welfare and multi-culturalism (Basu *et al.* 1992: 71).

These revivalists of the majority community are dragging in their communal stream a divergent following including *dalits*. These economically distressed and socially disabled people are being politically manipulated to serve the interests of caste Hindus in their effort to communalise society. Attempts are being made to ensure their presence in the Hindu niche in spite of it being inconvenient and repulsive to the *dalits*. 'Deceitful alleviation' of the *dalits* in the *Savarna* hierarchy is aimed at perpetuating the old social order in a new setting. The local and parochial religions of the *dalits* are being replaced by the absolutes from the Great Tradition, translated into a coherent set of metaphors, idioms and emotionally laden expressions. Fundamentalism seems to have accorded to the upper castes the role of *pater familias* seeking conformity to the traditional stratification system in which *dalits* have to be in a subservient state. They are being assimilated into the *Hindutva* dominated civil society. The sufferers are being transformed into sinners through the mechanism of providing them the hitherto denied access to the larger culture of the Hindu society. This paper is an attempt to study the response of the depressed classes to Hindu fundamentalism that has been on the offensive for the greater part of the last decade.

Dalits and the Fundamentalist Strategy

The fundamentalists have launched a multi-pronged strategy to consolidate their hold on the constituents of the Hindu community. The *Vishwa Hindu Parishad* (VHP) and the *Rashtriya Swayam Sevak Sangh* (RSS) have launched movements to reconvert the *dalits* from other religious groups. To illustrate how this is operative, we cite instances of *Prawartan* (return to the original position) as reported to be operative in Bihar:

> In a 400 km stretch from Simdega to Palamau in Bihar, the *Sri Banbasi Vikas Samiti* works assiduously to prevent people from being converted to Christianity..... Brahamchari Jayram Prapanna Maharaj has devised a novel method to stop Hindu conversions. For the past three years he has been organising a *Malviya Jayanti* on Christmas day to dissuade tribals from going to Church. The *Banbasi Kalyan Kendra*—an offshoot of the RSS—

was specially set up to wean tribals back to Hinduism. Headquartered at Lohardaga near Ranchi, the *Kendra* has established hospitals and temples for tribals and mounted a 'mass awareness campaign' during the Pope's visit to prevent conversions (Bhadwar 1986 : 81-82).

The conversion of a few Scheduled Caste people to Islam at Meenakshipuram in 1981 led to widespread unrest sponsored by the Hindu fundamentalist forces. Such conversions are projected by these elements as part of an international conspiracy against the Hindus. Through this they intend to maintain the traditional stratification pattern without removing the inner contradictions. Commenting on this strategy of the Hindu fundamentalists N.G. Gore, a leading socialist (quoted in Engineer 1986: 356), is reported to have observed:

> ....in the old days in order that the screams of a woman thrown on the burning pyre of her husband were not heard, the people around the pyre used to beat drums loudly. The VHP is similarly raising a hue and cry about the conversion of Scheduled Castes in Meenakkshipuram so that the people do not pay attention to the screams of the *dalits* burning on the pyre of discrimination.

Their preference for creation of a *Vananchal State* in Bihar by bringing together the districts inhabited by tribals is also a clear strategy directed against the Christians. To quote from a study of this movement:

> Behind the BJP's *Vananchal* movement is also a strategy to counter the growing influence of missionary activities in the tribal region. The missionaries have been converting the tribals to Christianity and have been a potent force behind the *Jharkhand* movement...... And simultaneously with the *Vananchal* campaign, the *Vanvasi Kalyan Kendra* (VKK)—an outfit of the BJP and RSS—has intensified its desire to reconvert the tribals to Hinduism. As a senior BJP leader confided, 'we cannot afford to let these missionaries turn the tribal region into *Chruchanchal*, hence a movement for *Vananchal* (Bharti 1989: 657).

It has to be noted that such reconversion to Hinduism has not meant status elevation to the Scheduled Castes or Tribes. In fact this makes them susceptible to such indignities that are experienced by them since time immemorial. To quote Thapar (1985:17):

> Hindu missionary organisations, taking their cue from Christian missionaries, are active among *adivasis,* untouchables and economically backward communities, converting them to 'Hinduism' as defined by the upper caste movements of the last two centuries. What is important to such missionaries is that these communities declare their support for the *dharma. That* this conversion does little or nothing to change their status as *adivasis,* untouchables and so on, and that they continue to be looked down upon by upper caste 'Hindus' is of course of little consequence.

Sanskritising the Dalit

'Sanskritisation', a process to ensure the upward mobility of individual castes in the caste hierarchy by imbibing the behaviour and practices of caste Hindus, has been a well known phenomenon in India.

> Sanskritisation is the process by which a low caste or tribe or other group takes over the customs, rituals, beliefs, ideology and style of a high, and in particular a twice born (*dwija)* caste. The Sanskritisation of a group has usually the effect of improving its position in the local caste hierarchy. It normally presupposes either an improvement in the economic position of the group concerned or a higher group self-consciousness resulting from its contact with a source of the Great Tradition of Hinduism such as a pilgrim centre or monastery or proselytising sect (Srinivas 1966:56).

In the past such attempts on the part of the untouchables and backward castes were not liked by the upper castes. In many cases such people were tortured for their attempts at Sanskritising themselves. In any case the positive orientation for reference and imitation of the upper caste values did not lead to any significant change in the status of the Scheduled Castes. Sanskritisation, thus, tends to represent a process of maintenance of the preordained status of the *dalits* in the caste hierarchy. It was a movement from below that had failed on account of the hostility of the upper castes.

The same strategy is being put to use by the forces of *Hindutva* to foster solidarity among the Hindus. This may be characterised as Sanskritisation from above, percolating downwards from the apex of the caste hierarchy. To provide an illustration we quote the situation as found to be operative in Tamil Nadu:

> *Rathams* run by the VHP have begun to symbolise Hindu unity drawing in Brahmins and the Scheduled Castes and even the supposedly Godless cadres of the *Dravida Munnetra Kazhahagam*. Three *Rathams* named *Shakti, Gyanam*, and *Deep* starting from villages in tamil Nadu criss-cross the south each day, carrying Hindu deities and *swamis* from various *muths* through villages and *Harijan bastis,* offering the lower castes the opportunity to perform *abhishek* which they are not allowed in the temples (Bhadwar 1986: 81-82).

In Saharanpur, the failure of the communal forces in ensuring the participation of *dalits* in riots on account of the *dalit*-Muslim alliance has led them to usher in a process of Sanskritising the *dalits.*

> The social and political future of Saharanpur depends on the form this conscious and nascent *dalit*-Muslim unity assumes. That on *Makar Sankranti* this year the BJP organised distribution of *Ram Khichdi* especially in the *Harijan Bastis* is probably a pointer that the *Hindutva* forces are not going to take this alliance lightly (Sujit and Indira 1993: 212).

A similar instance of Sanskritising non-Buddhist *dalits* is reported from Maharashtra and Gujarat. "....on the eve of the elections the BJP had invited *dalits* in Gujarat to participate in *Ram Shilanyas Pujas,* thereby drawing them into the support structure of the Hindu ideology" (Morkhandikar 1990: 587).

The laying of the first foundation stone at the temple site in Ayodhya was done by a *Harijan,* pressing him to the services of Lord Rama to help him to emerge as a reference model worth emulation by *dalits* elsewhere. *Dalits* are even made to fight for Lord Rama a privileged Hindus.

> A more fundamental motive seems to be the Hinduisation of (the) upwardly mobile sections from among the Bhangi caste through the test of rioting for Ram-a privilege that would incorporate them within a spiritual brotherhood without upsetting the material status quo. Similarly a *Harijan* was given the great privilege of laying the first foundation stone at the temple site in 1989. Symbolic solidarity is expected to overshadow the necessity of

practical solidarity. In fact, the VHP promotion of Valmiki group in particular is significant. It coordinates with Valmiki temple committees for its festivals. VHP literature pays obeisance to Valmiki and Ravi Das as Hindu religious leaders (Basu *et al.* 1992: 91-92).

The appointment of *Phalhari Baba*—a Chamar—as the chief priest of the famous Mahavir temple of Patna is also an invitation to *dalits* to Sanskritise their way of life without any hostility from the caste Hindus. As Bhelari (1993: 15) states,

> .....the appointment of Suryabansi, better known as *Phalhari Baba* because he takes nothing but fruits, was managed by the BJP which is keen on winning the *Harijans* over to its side. He was earlier the priest of the Ravidas temple of Ayodhya and among the dignitaries present when he took over as the chief priest were two stalwarts of the Ayodhya movement, Swami Avaidyanand of Gorakhpur *Math* and Paramhans Ramchandra Das of Ayodhya.....It is the first time a Harijan has been appointed the chief priest of any important temple in the country.

Similar moves by the Brahmins of Tamil Nadu are evident in their efforts to renovate an ancient temple of *Harijans:*

> In a gesture which can only be termed 'revolutionary' the Shankara *mutt* in Kanchipuram, a religious institution for centuries synonymous with Hindu caste orthodoxy, has undertaken to build a temple for a 5th century Tamil *Harijan* saint. Last week the head of this *mutt,* Shankaracharya Jayandra Saraswathi, laid the foundation stone and himself performed the *Bhoomi Pooja* or the pre-construction earth worshipping rite for a temple for the *Harijan* saint Nandannar, at Aadhanoor near the famous temple of Chidambaram, south of Madras. The Acharya announced that this *mutt* would bear the entire cost of the temple to be built, befitting Nandannar's great sacrifice for the cause of equality (Anon 1993).

Integration in Mainstream Hinduism

These incidents provide illustrations of caste Hindu manipulations aimed at the Sanskritisation of the *dalits* to serve the designs of the fundamentalist forces. The symbolic elevation, cannot even be a substitute for sincere attempts at real integration of the *dalits* with the caste Hindus. It is a political design to obtain a strong communal support base. Untouchability still remains an essential of Hinduism. Discrimination against them tends to be tenacious. The resource disadvantage of *dalits* tends to remain by and large cumulative. Anticipation of diminution of power on account of erosion in the traditionally legitimised position in society has led the caste Hindus to raise communal issues.

> The campaign of the Hindu unity is actually directed against the Muslims.... The perpetrators of the status quo...need the spectre of an external enemy to beat into submission the have-nots within. The RSS...has mastered the game of using the threat from fast breeding aggressive Muslims to suppress the internal contradictions of Hindu society and keep the Scheduled Castes in perpetual bondage (Engineer 1991: 357).

Hindu fundamentalism got sharpened under the threat from the *dalits* involved in an extensive protest network. Such mobilisation of peasants, tribals and *dalits* challenged the bastion of political authority traditionally controlled by the upper caste Hindus. Their newly found concern at the sad plight of these 'wretched of the earth' is primarily out of political exigency and is not because their guilty conscience has been stirred.

> ....it was not Ram but threat to their own privilege that made them and their Hinduism go militant. It is their interests which mobilised *sadhus* and religious leaders of various Hindu sects on such a gigantic scale never seen before in the modern history of Hinduism. In fact, in a number of constituencies in UP the *sadhus* who were never involved in politics earlier, campaigned for the BJP candidates. We thus witnessed unprecedented use of religion for political purpose by these upper caste Hindus. The *Shiv Sena* and VHP even distributed *trishuls* in Bombay and elsewhere during the election campaign (ibid).

In the tribal areas it is the *dikus*—the tribal term for non-tribals and outsiders—that intend to protect or ensure their continued exploitation, who constitute the core of fundamentalist support. In order to weaken any attempt to forge *dalit* corporate identity, fundamentalist parties and outfits seem to have applied different strategies. Important among them is the Hinduisation of the heros of the *dalit* movements. This has happened in Maharashtra.

> At the theoretical level the BJP is trying to (mis) interpret Ambedkar's mode of thinking and argues that his act of conversion was in conformity with Hinduism rather than its subversion. Also these neo-Hindu forces are attempting the convenient comparison of Ambedkar with Hedgewar and Savarkar and are showing how all these three tried to create a common Hindu identity by fighting against the bad practice of caste and untouchability (Guru 1991: 339).

Active participation in Ambedkar celebrations, formation of social assimilation organisations for the integration of the untouchables with the caste Hindus, and providing positions of importance to *dalit* youth connected with RSS and ABVP, appear to be other strategies used by the Hindu fundamentalist forces to carve out a niche for themselves among the *dalits.*

In situations where the *dalits* are opposed to the forces of *Hindutva,* attempts are reported to have been made to exclude such *dalits* from the emerging fundamentalist support structure. Such *dalits* are often targets of atrocities perpetrated by caste Hindus. There is an attempt to win such sections among the *dalits* who are not opposed to *Hindutva.* For example.

> ....the *Shiv Sena* in Maharashtra has adopted a new strategy to win over *dalits* into their scheme of Hinduisation of *dalits*. It is evident from the *Shiv Sena's* crude condemnation of Ambedkar and its threat of physical liquidation to the Mahar-neo-Buddhist combine, that it intends to single out for persecution those groups who, by and large, are the followers of Ambedkar and his Buddhism. But it is trying to co-opt other *dalits* such as Mangs, Chambhars and Dhors who are by and more inclined towards Hinduism. The *Shiv Sena* does this co-option by absorbing these sections into its organisational structure and certain other opportunity structures which it happens to control in the State.

Intra-community cleavages among *dalits* provide a powerful spur to the fundamentalist forces to isolate them for future co-option to their fold. We cite the case of Aurangabad Municipality elections where lack of cohesion among *dalits* is posing a threat to the strength of their protest movement:

> Earlier, in the elections (1988) held for the Aurangabad Municipal Corporation, the BRP (Bhartiya Republican Party) had won one and the Panthers two seats. Had they fought the elections under a united banner, it was argued, the *dalits* could have won at least 20 seats. The major beneficiary was their arch-rival, the *Shiv Sena.* The threat from BJP-*Sena* was not only to the *dalit* organisations, but Ambedkarism itself seemed endangered (Morkandikar 1990: 587).

In recent years the attempts to induct *dalits* into the fundamentalists' support structure has been accorded much more emphasis. Their sudden concern for atrocities on tribals in Rajasthan is indicative of fresh political strategies aimed at the recruitment of the *dalits* to the saffron fold.

> ...what seems intriguing is the BJP's ultimatum to the State Government that it would hold a massive demonstration before the Prime Minister if a "Judicial inquiry was not ordered by tomorrow (July 7th, 1993) into the police atrocities on tribals..." Observers have question why the BJP had not reacted strongly against the incident in May itself (Anon 1993a).

Creating a Vote Bank

This and many other similar incidents are instances of politics of aggregation being pursued by the fundamentalist forces to cast their net as wide as possible to strengthen their support base. The social charter released after the latest meeting of the BJP national bodies puts emphasis on the party's commitment to the ideal of a socially integrated society as the very basis for the sustenance of India as a modern dynamic nation. All socially and economically weaker sections of society have been promised help through 'social welfare and other schemes to reach their potential for contribution to their society and accord them an honoured place in society' (Anon 1993b).

The attempts of the fundamentalist forces aimed at forging a broad Hindu identity for political gains has to take into account the *dalits* whose number is an important source of power. Caste Hindus on their own cannot capture power. They have to activate the forces of religion in order to build a network comprising cross sections among the Hindu population including *dalits*. This is what has been called quite interestingly the *dhobi factor*.

> ...*dhobis* (washermen) had forced Lord Ram to part company with Sita after the Lord's triumphant return from Lanka. And according to the Ramayana all this happened in Ayodhya. Ram had listened to the *dhobi* because the latter was not just a *dhobi*. He represented the voice of the people.

Herein lies the importance of the *dhobi factor* in politics. The *Bharatiya Janata Party* leadership appears to have suddenly realised that the *dhobi factor* is more important than Ram even in the twentieth century. And in the final decade of the twentieth century the *dhobi* stands for OBCs and *dalits* (Sahay 1993).

In its recent reshuffling, the apex body of the *Bharatiya Janata Party* has inducted Suraj Bhan (Scheduled Caste), Karia Munda (Scheduled Tribe) and Klayan Singh (OBC) as Vice-Presidents. In Uttar Pradesh it claims substantial support of Kurmi, Odhi, Pal, Gujjar, Saini, Kewat, Mallah, Nishad, Bind, Nai, Kumhar and Swarankar. These are mainly distressed groups among the intermediate Castes. Efforts are on to split the Yadavas (Anon 1993c). In Bihar the central leadership's intent to 'provide' the President of its State wing from among one of the backward castes failed in the wake of manipulation at the local level (Anon 1993). In Madhya Pradesh the BJP is claiming to be more concerned about the backwards than the Congress (Anon 1993d). Stirring up the temple issue has helped the BJP in the saffronisation of the intermediate castes. In dissolved Assembly of Uttar Pradesh, 33 per cent of the BJP members were from the backward castes. Apart from Kalyan Singh, a Lodh, the other "leading backward lights of the Ram movement include Vinay Katiyar, a kurmi, and Sadhvi Ritambhara, a Lodh, apart from Uma Bharti, also a Lodh from Madhya Pradesh" (Mukerji and Bhelari 1993: 14).

This is also true of *Shiv Sena* especially in Madhya Pradesh. A study of *Shiv Sainiks* in Chattisgarh reveals that the bulk is constituted of upper castes. However, also the presence of the intermediate and lower castes is reported.

> The majority of the Sena's members belong to the higher castes, with Brahmins and Rajputs constituting more than half from the so called 'backward castes', especially Yadavas who are not poorly represented, and members of mercantile castes (Sahus). The *Shiv Sena* exerts a certain appeal on the members of several minorities, persons originally from Maharashtra, young Sikhs, members of the Sindhi community, and recently members of very low castes who have come from the adjacent States of Bihar and Orissa (Heuze 1992: 2190).

Accomplices in Communal Riots

Reports of recent communal riots reveal a tendency on the part of *dalits* to be accomplices in the rabid manifestations of fundamentalism. They are also in a few cases infected by the communal virus. For example, a report on the riots in Delhi in 1984 maintains :

> The team members, on the basis of extensive interviews in different parts of the city, were able to piece together the characteristics of the mobs that were responsible for the looting, arson and killings. In some cases the mobs were brought from outside the locality. They were transported in vehicles. A large number of Scheduled Caste people were also a part of the marauding groups (Anon 1984: 1979).

Their involvement in the communal riots is reported to be sponsored by the upper caste leaders. They have been offered monetary incentives for their participation in the riots. To corroborate one can cite excerpts from a report on the communal riots in Meerut in 1982:

> In Meerut... the caste Hindus had used members of the Valmiki community (Bhangis or sweepers) who are extremely poor, to fight the Muslims. It was rumoured... that Valmikis were paid Rs 200 and a bottle of liquor for killing one Muslim... According to Smt. Harpal Singh, the former MLA from Meerut, Mohanlal Kapoor who belongs to the BJP, nowadays comes to meerut from a long distance to perform *puja* along with *dalits*. This is a calculated move to split the votes which have normally gone in favour of Congress (I). It is also interesting that generally only the poor and illiterate Valmikis have fallen for the RSS game, not the Chamars who are more educated and conscious (Engineer 1982a: 1803).

In the post-Ayodhya riots in Surat the participation of the poor working class Hindu labourers from middle range and Scheduled Castes is corroborated (Breman 1992: 739). The *Hindutva* forces' claim of communal friendship with the *dalits* in the recent riots of Bombay provides further evidence of their success in mobilising the *dalits* for communal ends. Speaking about the situation in Gujarat, Engineer (1993: 262) says :

> Over the years, the influence of the traditional upper caste Vanias and Brahmins has declined and the middle castes like Kambis, Khatris, Glanchi and Gola Ranas have emerged as the dominant group... It is the emergent middle classes and castes among the Hindus which are aggressively asserting their domination. The BJP has offered them an ideology and powers of articulation.

In Sitamarhi, Bihar, there are reports of widespread participation of Scheduled Castes and Backwards in the communal riots last year. On occasions, the fundamentalist forces spread wild rumors to rupture the alliance and solidarity of the *dalit*-Muslim constellation. For example,

> The situation in some villages to the north of Saharanpur city was different. The demolition of the mosque was celebrated by some belonging to the upper castes. Further, attempts were made by them to foment fights between the *dalits* (mainly of the Chamar community) and Muslims. For instance, the Chamars in a number of villages were informed of the destruction of the Ravidas temple (place of worship of Chamars) at such and such places by the Muslims... Not only did the Chamars not get carried away by the rumours, they took the lead in protecting some mosques from *goonda* elements (Sujit and Indira 1993: 212).

These bits of evidence indicate that the *dalits* have never initiated a riot. They, however, do not remain insulated and at times participate in the riots, killing and plundering people who are proximate to their social status. They act as affiliates to upper or middle castes in the communal riots. This is attributed to the 'overpowering Hindu ethos' and to the contradictions within the locality shared by the two communities.

The role of *dalits* in communal riots has corroborated from the evidence from Moradabad, Aligarh, Old Delhi, Hyderabad, Bhiwandi and other places (Engineer 1992: 2463). However, the role of middle range castes in planning and executing such riots cannot be denied. One such instance is the riots of Badaun. The leadership provided by a Kurmi politician in those riots of 1989 led to widespread communalism among other middle range castes of the area. The same is the story of Bhagalpur and Biharsharif in Bihar.

Conclusion

To conclude, fundamentalism, as manifested in the concept of *Hindutva*, represents efforts at social mobilisation to achieve political ends. It represents a case of manipulating the religious identity of the *dalits* for political purposes. It does not indicate sincere efforts for fundamental changes in the Hindu society. Rather, it is oriented to the strengthening of the status quo. Its aim is to induct *dalits* as 'affiliates' to the forces of fundamentalism, and has serious implications for the emergence of a corporate identity among them. The emergence of autonomous protest movements and a strong *dalit* identity have been crippled on account of the 'politics of aggregation' effectively used by the ruling caste Hindus to lull the stirrings of discontent among the *dalits*, into a deep slumber. Fundamentalism has still wider implications for society, and more particularly for the *dalits*. They have to become aware of and have to expose the deceitful and pernicious designs of the divisive forces. The efforts at 'symbolic unity' are a cruel device to perpetuate the exploitation of the depressed. This is an effort to subvert the emergence of any autonomous ideology and identity among the *dalits*. Such fundamentalist designs have to be prevented if a new identity is to emerge out of the slow awakening of the *dalits*.

REFERENCES

Anon. 1984. "Who are the Guilty?-Causes and Impact of the Delhi Riots," *Economic and Political Weekly*, 19 (n.47, November 24), pp. 1979-1985.

—.1993. News Item, *The Hindustan Times* (Patna Edition), July 8.

—. 1993a. News Item, *The Times of India*, (New Delhi), July 6.

—. 1993b. News Item, *The Times of India*, (New Delhi), June 20.

—. 1993c. News Item, *The Hindustan Times* (Patna Edition), July 3.

—. 1993d. News Item, *The Times of India*, (New Delhi), July 24.

Basu, Tapan et al. 1992. *Khaki Shorts, Saffron Flags*. New Delhi: Orient Longmans Limited.

Bhadwar, Inderjit. 1986. "Millitant Revivalism," *India Today*, May 31, pp. 80-82.

Bharti, Indu. 1989. "Bihar: Behind BJP's Vananchal Demand," *Economic and Political Weekly*, 24 (n.13, April 1), pp. 656-657.

Bhelari, Kanhaiah. 1993. "Acid Sermons," *The Week*, July 25, pp. 14-15.

Breman, Jan. 1993. "Anti-Muslim Program in Surat," *Economic and Political Weekly*, 28 (n. 16, April 17), pp. 737-741.

Engineer, Asghar Ali. 1982. "Maharashtra: Behind the Communal Fury," *Economic and Political Weekly*, 17 (n. 10, March 6), pp. 356-357.

—. 1982a. "Uttar Pradesh: The Guilty Men of Meerut," *Economic and Political Weekly*, 17 (n.45, November 6), pp.1803-1807.

—. 1991. "Lok Sabha Elections and Communalisation of Politics," *Economic and Political Weekly*, 26 (n. 27-28, July 6), pp. 1649-1652.

—. 1992. "Sitamarhi on Fire," *Economic and Political Weekly*, 27 (n. 46, November 14), pp. 2462-2464.

—. 1993. "Bastion of Communal Amity Crumbles," *Economic and Political Weekly*, 28 (n 7, February 13), pp. 262-264.

Gould, Harold A. 1993. "Fascism Wrapped in Saffron Robe," *The Times of India*, (New Delhi), July 1.

Guru, Gopal. 1991. "Hinduisation of Ambedkar in Maharashtra," *Economic and Political Weekly*, 26 (n. 7, February 16), pp. 339-341.

Khare, Harish. 1986. "Fundamentalism, "*Seminar* (n 322, June), pp. 14-18.

Heuze, Gerard. 1992. "Shiv Sena and 'National' Hinduism," *Economic and Political Weekly*, 27 (n. 10, October 3), pp. 2189-2195.

Morkhandikar, R.S. 1990. "Dilemmas of Dalit Movement in Maharashtra: Unity Moves and After," *Economic and Political Weekly*, 25 (n. 12, March 24), pp. 586-590.

Mukerji, Debashish and Khanhaiah Bhelari. 1993. 'Changing Colour,' *The Week*, May 2, pp 14-15.

Sahay, Ambika Nand. 1993. *The Times of India*, July 4.

Srinivas, M.N. 1966. *Social Change in Modern India and Other Essays*. Bombay: Allied Publishers.

Sujit and Indira. 1993. "Saharanpur : Post-Demolition Situation," *Economic and Political Weekly*, 28 (n. 6, February 6), p. 212.

Talib, Rasheed. 1993. "Hindutva : Flattery by Imitation," *Seminar*, (n. 402, February), pp. 37-39.

Thapar, Romila. 1985. "Syndicated Moksha?" *Seminar* (n. 313, September), pp 14-22.

13

UNIFORM CIVIL CODE

Nil Ratan

The word 'secular' was added to the preamble of Indian Constitution during the 1975-1977 period, but till date it remains to be defined. Gandhi's view of secularism was '*sarvdharma sambhav*'. India's first Prime Minister Pundit Jawahar Lal Nehru agreed with Gandhi's view and wrote, 'A secular state does not obviously mean a state where religion is discouraged. It means freedom of religion and conscience, including freedom for those who have no religion, subject only to their not interfering with each other, with the basic conception of our state. Article 25 (1) gives fundamental right for "freedom of conscience and right to freely profess, practise and propagate religion". The basic feature of secularism as it is understood in the West is that there will be no discrimination between citizens on the basis of their religion or forms of worship and that everybody will be equal before the law.

India ceases to be secular for it has different sets of laws for different communities; for the Muslims, for instance, separate Civil Code exists, though Article 44 requires the state to frame a uniform Civil Code. S. Gopal[1] remarks that Nehru in his keenness to win the confidence of the Muslim community failed to ensure the equality before law of all Indians and enact a common Civil Code. Religion can be separated from politics more easily if it is also separated from the law. There is no room in a secular society for differences in personal law which claims religious sanction. To deny rights to Muslim women which are available to women of other faith is a violation of the provision in the Constitution that the state shall not discriminate against any citizen on grounds of religion.

The controversy of Uniform Civil Code is nothing new to India as after independence time and again it has been raised, sometimes by citizens' forum, and sometimes by judiciary. Once again this issue has sprung into prominence because of judgements delivered by Justice Kuldip Singh & Justice Sahai in their special leave petitions. The judgements are reported in Sarla Mudgal & others V/s Union of India (1995) 3 S.C.C. 635. The common question raised by the three petitions was, is marriage between persons professing the same religion dissolved if one of them becomes a convert to another religions. Obviously this question has to be decided under the Constitution and does not raise any question about a common Civil Code and the two judges held likewise and dismissed the petitions.

Before going further into the controversy it is better to have a historical look about the issue. The Muslim Personal Laws (Shariat) Act were enacted by the British in 1937[2]. With its enactment its in-built drawback was started being misused by the people. With the controversy arising every now and then the Indian National Congress appointed National Planning Committee for political debate of Uniform Civil Code in 1940.

The directive to enact it was included in the Indian Constitution by the efforts of Minoo Masani. Being a member of the Constituent Assembly Sub-committee on Fundamental Rights, Masani proposed on March 28, 1947 that the state should be made responsible for enacting a uniform civil code to break down the barriers between various communities. While Masani, Hansa Mehta, Rajkumari Amrit Kaur, Dr. B. R. Ambedkar voted in favour of a constitutional clause on Uniform Civil Code but a majority of the sub-committee members voted against it on the ground that it was beyond the scope of fundamental rights. However, the sub-committee agreed to make the enactment of a Uniform Civil Code a Directive Principle of state policy, mainly to allay Muslim fears.[3]

So this is how uniform Civil Code became a part of Directive Principles of State Policy instead of Fundamental Rights of the Constitutional and came in Part IV instead of Part III. So under Art. 44 it reads as follows : "The State shall endeavour to secure for the citizens a Uniform Civil Code throughout the territory of India".

However let us make it clear that Part IV of the Constitution i.e., Directive Principles of State Policy (Arts. 36-51) is not justifiable. As according to Art. 37, the provisions contained in this part shall not be enforceable by any court, but the principles therein laid down are nevertheless fundamental in the governance of the country and it shall be the duty of the state to apply these principles in making laws.

So here comes the matter of basic structure of the Constitution and the conflict of Fundamental Rights guaranteed to citizens (obviously including minorities (U/A 25,26, 27, 28 and specially to minorities U/A 29 and 30 with that of Directive Principles of State Policy U/A 44 (U.C.C.).

After the Constitution was adopted, the state continued with the codification and reform of the Hindu personal laws but did not touch the personal laws of minorities. Against the forces of the group opposing the UCC Dr. B. R. Ambedkar in 1953 said that a secular state did not mean that it could flout the sentiments of the people. In the provisional parliament, and subsequently in the first Lok Sabha, the Government stood by its stand that the Hindu Code Bill was but the first step towards a UCC[4].

However on the point of enactment of Hindu Code Bill in 1956 a controversy arose between Nehru and Rajen Babu. While Rajen Babu's[5] approach was more futuristic for the governance of the country, Nehru's view was that time was ripe. He was thinking in terms of Congress's gain rather than national interest. On the point of Hindu Code Bill, Rajen Babu had asked Dr. Ambedkar about his personal opinion. He reiterated his old stand of UCC and asked about reforming all the personal laws and why Hindu's code only.

Rajen Babu was quite satisfied with Ambedkar's opinion and advised Nehru to reform and implement the personal laws on the wholesome basis to bring unity and uniformity in the country but Nehru took stiff stand on his decision and with the help of majority he led the Hindu Code Bill, thus the Act was passed by the Parliament, then Rajen Babu had no other choice but to sign it. The Hindu Code Bill 1956 included :

— The Special Marriage Bill
— The Hindu Marriage Bill
— The Hindu Succession Bill

— The Hindu Minority and Guardianship Bill
— The Hindu Maintenance and Adoption Bill

After that there was no significant activity on the part of the state to initiate the process of enacting a Uniform Civil Code, until the Shah Bano case controversy erupted. When the Government introduced the Muslim Women Bill in the Lok Sabha in 1986, it was accused of succumbing to the pressure of Muslim fundamentalists[6]. On this pretext Arif Mohammed Khan had resigned claiming ulemas as orthodox and Muslim world as non-progressive. To counter the charge Prime Minister Rajiv Gandhi said that Government would introduce a UCC Bill in the following session of Parliament. However it was not introduced owing to fears expressed in various quarters. In Shah Bano Case Sec. 125 of Cr. P. C. had come into conflict with the Muslim Personal Law. The Supreme Court rejected this contention upon the interpretation of Section 125, namely that it applied to all persons, irrespective of their religion and personal law and dismissed the husbands' appeal.

Delivering the judgement Chief Justice Y. V. Chandrachud observed that it was a "matter of regret" that the state had not made any attempt to make a Uniform Civil Code even though Art. 44 existed.[7] As a learned professor of the Bombay University Professor Siddiqui observed if the State took the lead, ultimately the Muslim Community would accept it because it was in accordance with the notion of modernised society.

Overriding the clear observations of the Supreme Court and rejecting the protests of a large section of the Muslim Community including learned scholars, the Congress Government enacted the Muslim Women (Protection of Rights & Divorce) Act 1986 providing that the statutory provision contained in this Act should govern unless the divorced woman and her former husband apply to the court that they would prefer to be governed by the provisions of section 125 Cr. P. C. as to the right of maintenance of the divorced wife.

The Congress government was criticised by progressive Muslims including Arif Mohammed Khan, a prominent Congress minister and a close friend of then Prime Minister Rajiv Gandhi, who had resigned on this issue. According to them, the Congress government had thus paved way to the Muslim fundamentalists to violate the Supreme Court decisions as well as the Constitution, which directs the state to make a Uniform Civil Code, overriding any personal law to the contrary. The National Front Government also took the stand that there would be no Uniform Civil Code unless the minority community wanted it.

Thus, an opportunity created by Shah Bano Case Judgement for upliftment of minorities women was lost by Government of India, hence the parity which would have come for minority women all the other women was deprived.

Another legal verdict came from the Kerala High Court when on February 24, 1995 it struck down any unjust provision of the Indian Divorce Act 1869, an exclusively Christian law. The law on marriage for the Christians in India is regulated by the Indian Christian Marriage Act 1872. However it is not applicable in the erstwhile State of Travancore-Cochin, Manipur and Jammu & Kashmir where the local customs and practices are prevalent among the community in that area i.e. the Canon Laws and other personal laws are applicable.

Regarding divorce, the law applicable to Christians throughout the country (except Jammu and Kashmir) is Indian Divorce Act. The application of the provisions of the Indian Christian Marriage Act and the Indian Divorce Act has created difficulties as they clash with Christian Personal Law. According to section 10 of the Act, the Civil Courts could allow a divorce for a man on the ground that his wife was guilty of adultery, but not for a woman whose husband was guilty of the same offence. The wife would be granted freedom from a marriage only if the husband was found guilty of incestuous adultery or of bigamy with adultery or of marriage with another woman with adultery coupled with cruelty or of adultery coupled with discretion so the court (H.C.C. J.M.M. Prareed Pillay, J.T.V. Ramakrishnan and J. P. Shanmugum) upheld the contention of the two writ petitions regarding divorce and stated that some of the provisions of Section 10 of the Indian Divorce Act were violative of Arts. 14, 15 and 21 of the Constitution, thus the judgement made it possible for a Christian woman to seek dissolution of her marriage on any one of the grounds of adultery, cruelty and desertion in parity with women of large communities.

Similarly, a divorce sanctioned by the religious courts would not be legally valid unless and until it was sanctioned by a Civil Court, thus Civil laws have precedence over canonical law in Christian marriages. These developments have been welcomed largely by minority Christian Community.

The Sarla Mudgil and Others *Vs.* Union of India (1995) 3 S.C.C. 635 after Shah Bano Case has once again revived the debate for Uniform Civil Code. The Supreme Court on May 10 Judgement held that the second marriage of a Hindu husband after conversion to Islam, without having the first marriage dissolved under law, would be invalid.[8] The petitioner represented the deserted wives of four men. The Supreme Court held that the second marriage between the apposite and his Hindu wife is the transgression of the Hindu Marriage Act and would be as such non-existent and void marriage in terms of section 494 of the Indian Penal Code which deals with bigamy and even though the husband has adopted Islam, the marriage would be treated under the Hindu Marriage Act. It struck down the right assumed by Hindu husbands to practise polygamy under the cover of converting to Islam. The court nullified the second marriage of their husbands. This ruling affects the right of convert only. A born Muslim can still have four wives, as permitted by the Muslim Personal Law (Shariat) Application Act enacted by the British in 1937. The Supreme Court suggested that the personal law of the minorities should be rationalized in order to promote cultural amity. Mr. Justice Kuldip Singh pointed out that the personal laws of the Hindus relating to marriage, succession and the like have all a sacramental origin in the same manner as in the case of the Muslims or the Christians. He said that it is not necessary to have connection between religion and personal law in a civilized society. Justice Kuldip Singh and Justice R. M. Sahai observed that "Till the time we achieve the goal of Uniform Civil Code for all the citizens of India—there is an open inducement to a Hindu husband, who wants to enter into a second marriage while the first marriage is subsisting to become a Muslim"[9].

The Supreme Court in its judgement has requested the government through the Prime Minister to have a "Fresh Look"[10] at Article 44 of the Constitution mandating the state to secure a Uniform Civil Code for the citizens throughout the territory of India.

"The successive governments till date have wholly failed in their duty of implementing the constitutional mandate under Article 44 of the Constitution of India", observed Mr. Justice Kuldip Singh and Mr. Justice R. M. Sahai. The Judges directed the secretary, Ministry of Law and Justice, to file an affidavit of a responsible officer in the apex court by August 1996, indicating therein the steps taken and efforts made by the Union of India towards securing a "Uniform Civil Code" for the citizens. The Judges said that the desirability of a Uniform Civil Code could hardly be doubted but it could be concretised only when the social climate was popularly built up by the elite of the society."

"Today it is unfortunate that there is no Raja Ram Mohan Roy who single-handedly brought about the atmosphere which paved the way for the abolition of *Sati* nor is there a statesman of the stature of Pandit Nehru who could pilot successfully the Hindu Succession Act and the Hindu Marriage Act revolutionising the Constitution-made Hindu law", Justice Sahai said. The problem today was that many Hindus had changed their religion and had converted to Islam for the sole purpose of escaping the consequences of bigamy. "But no religion permits deliberate distortions. Much apprehension prevails about bigamy in Islam itself with many Islamic countries codifying their personal law to check its misuse", the Judges said adding that India being a secular democratic republic even the slightest deviation shook the social fabric. The Judges said the first step in a Uniform Civil Code was to rationalize the personal law of the minorities to develop religious and cultural amity. The government would be well advised to entrust the responsibility in this regard to the law commission, examine the matter and bring about the comprehensive legislation in keeping with modern day concept of human rights for women.

In his separate judgement, Mr. Justice Kuldip Singh said one wondered how long it would take the government of the day to implement the mandate of the Constitution under Article 44. Justice Kuldip Singh said the political history of India showed that during the Muslim regime, justice was administered by the quazis who would obviously apply Muslim scriptural law to Muslims. But there was no similar assurance so far as litigations concerning Hindus were concerned.

So far as the criminal justice was concerned the British gradually superseded Muslim law in 1832 and it came to be governed by the English Common Law. Finally the Indian Penal Code was enacted in 1860.

Justice Kuldip Singh held that a Common Civil Code did not violate the freedom of religion guaranteed by Articles 25, 26 and 27 of Indian Constitution. On this point, Justice Sahai dissented and referred to Supreme Court decisions which had held that religion was not merely a matter of faith and belief but included rituals, ceremonies and prayers in temples, mosques, and Churches etc. But on the question of whether a common Civil Code would violate freedom of religion, Justice Sahai did not concur.

Now after this judgement, a national debate has stirred for those supporting a Uniform Civil Code or opposing a Uniform Civil Code.

H. M. Seervai says that both judges inadvertently overlooked Article 14(5) which provides that no judgement shall be delivered in the Supreme Court except with the concurrence of a majority of judges hearing the case. Since the two judges differed as aforesaid, they could deliver no judgement at all on the point whether a common code did or did not violate the freedom of religion. According to Seervai, the Supreme Court cannot enforce the mandate of Article 44, consequently the aforesaid order is null and void. It is not the judiciary but the executive which can consider what law should be submitted to parliament and it is the latter which alone can decide whether or not to enact a proposed law. He says those who have studied Hindu law and Mohammedan law will realise that a common Civil Code for Hindus and Muslims is an impossibility.[11]

Seervai analysing the Mohammedan law comments that the Mohammedans are divided into two sects and sub-sects, the two sects being Sunnis and Shias. Sunnis are divided into four sub-sects, namely, the Hanafis, the Malikis, the Shafeis and the Hababs. The Mohammedan law applicable to each sect or sub-sect is to prevail as the litigants of that sect or sub-sect (Mulla's Mohammedan Law; 19th edn. pp 20-21, 1990). It is clear therefore that "Mohammedan law" does not uniformly apply to all Mohammedans. Seervai says that common Civil Code is a mirage.

According to M. Hasmi Kidwai, Uniform Civil Code is an attempt to destroy the religious and cultural practices of minorities and this will set in motion a very dangerous precedent. According to him, Muslim Personal Law has for centuries pioneered the following progressive principles: That marriage is a Civil Contract involving no change in the legal status of the woman, the wife's retention of her full legal personality with plenary capacity to contract and to acquire, hold and dispose of property with reference to her husband, the wife's right to demand from her husband as an essential precondition of marriage, a settlement or *mehr* (dower). The wife's right to *hizamat* i.e. custody of young children in case of separation from her husband with the latter remaining liable for maintenance. The woman's right to remarry after divorce on widowhood. The woman's right to stipulate conditions for marriage contract. Thus, he argues that the enforcement of Article 44 will be against the basic structure of the Constitution.[12]

Syed Shahabuddin has given a set of reasons of Muslim objections to a common civil code. First, the assurance about non-interference in Muslim personal law in independent India was not a personal assurance by Gandhi and Nehru but written into the resolutions of the Indian National Congress since the twenties. Secondly, that all Muslim members of the Constituent Assembly opposed the provision of uniform Civil Code and demanded exception for the Muslim Community on the ground of freedom of religion and of conscience. According to him, the Muslim objection is to a motivated and determined endeavour to destroy their religious identity, to undermine the essentials of the faith-commitment to the *Quran* as the word of God and to assimilate them. He says that there is no equation between uniformity and unity in a plural society, in a situation of religious and cultural diversity. Even the Hindu Code is not uniform, it allows exception. And the introduction of a Common Civil Code is not a question which affects Muslims and other religious minorities only but also all tribal groups and others governed by their customary laws.[13]

There are those who expound moderate views and talk of revamping personal laws but they do not agree to imposition of a Uniform Civil Code.

According to Surendra Mohan, no one can take exception to evolve a common code by the willing consensus of all sections of society. But such a code will then have to be based on rational and modern concepts of equality between the sexes. The willing consent of either spouse to marry the other, a consent of both parties in respect of divorce, total banning of dowry and *mehr*, complete monogamy, equal rights in respect of adoption and equal rights in property would have to form the basis of such a code.[14]

E. M. S. Namboodiripad writes that the Community itself should take the initiative and reform its personal law. According to Asghar Ali Engineer, the State should refrain from implementation of Uniform Civil Code. He asked the ulemas to consider the question of reforming the Muslim personal law. He points out that while many existing Muslim personal laws in India called the Shariat are opposed to the principles laid down in the *Koran*, many others included in the Muslim personal law, though conforming to the *Koran*, are no more valid in present day conditions. Engineer suggests that instead of Indian Parliament codifying the common Civil Code applicable to all communities, the Muslim community, through its theologians, should take the initiative for reforming the existing Muslim personal law in order to make it conform to the norms and principles of modern progressive democracy.[15]

The position of Uniform Civil Code in Islamic countries is strong and the countries like Syria, Tunisia, Morocco, Pakistan, Iran and the Islamic republics of the former Soviet Union have codified personal laws to check its abuse and have banned polygamy.[16]

The political parties in India have their own views of the common code. The Bhartiya Janata Party wants its implementation without delay and has been a consistent advocate for Uniform Civil Code. Recently, two BJP-run state governments are trying to re-define Article 246 in connection with definition of state and they want to implement Uniform Civil Code in their states i.e. Gujarat and Maharashtra respectively. Prime Minister P.V. Narasimha Rao on August 15, 1995 Independence day speech made it absolutely clear that the state does not have the implementation of Uniform Civil Code on its agenda, hence the Congress position is self-evident.[17]

The latest position is that the Supreme Court has just clarified that its May 10 recommendation of a Uniform Civil Code is only 'obiter dicta',[18] thus not mandatory on the state to implement Uniform Civil Code nor is it binding for the state now to come prepared within one year as to what has been done on the issue.

Where do we go from here now? The position of a just, equitable civil society is measured by the equal rights it gives to its citizens irrespective of caste, colour, creed, race and sex. The position of women needs to be strengthened in all the communities, hence the debate for reforms in personal laws by communities must be vigorously pursued for their social emancipation. The society today needs the likes of Sir Syed Ahmed Khan, Raja Ram Mohan Roy, Ishwar Chand Vidyasagar etc. to lead the social reforms movement in their respective communities to promote equity and just, rational society, without threatening the multi-cultural plural identities, because India's unity lies in its diversities.

REFERENCES

1. Nehru and Minorities, S. Gopal, *Economic and Political Weekly,* Vol. XXIII, special Number, 1988.
2. Striking down a Right, Manoj Mitta, *India Today,* p. 118, June 15, 1995.
3. A law for Act, V. Venkatesan, *Frontline,* June 16, 1995, p. 41.
4. An Elusive Affair, V. Venkatesan, *Frontline*, June 16, 1995, p. 42.
5. Uniform Civil Code, *Rashtriya Sahara,* Saturday, 3 June, 1995, p. 8.
6. *Ibid.,* V. Venkatesan, June 16, 1995, p. 41.
7. Why conflicting voices? Vijay Kumar Malhotra, *Hindustan Times,* Patna, August 5, 1995, p. 7.
8. *Ibid.,* p. 41, June 16, 1995.
9. *Ibid.,* p. 118, Manoj Mitta, June 15, 1995.
10. *Ibid.,* p. 41, June 16, 1995.
11. Uniform Civil Code, H.M. Seervai, *Times of India,* July 5, 1995.
12. Muslim Personal Law, H. Hasmi Kidwai, *Times of India,* July 31, 1995.
13. Muslim Stand on Civil Code, Syed Shahbuddin, *Mainstream,* August 5, 1995.
14. BJP Shiva Sena's New Zeal for Common Code, Surendra Mohan, *Mainstream*, July 15, 1995, pp. 5-6.
15. The Civil Code debate, E.M.S. Namboodripad, *Frontline,* July 14, 1995, p. 104.
16. *Ibid.,* V. Ventakesh, p. 47, June 16, 1995.
17. *Hindustan Times*, Patna, August 17, 1995.
18. Revamping Personal Laws, August 17, *Times of India*, Patna, p. 6.

14

PHILOSOPHICAL PERSPECTIVE OF SECULARISM

Suresh Prasad

Prefatory Note

The all-pervasive social, economic, political and cultural crisis due to unequal, irrational and inhuman capitalistic path of development that has been engulfing the country more and more in recent decades is spreading moods of insecurity, pessimism, cynicism, and loss of faith among vast mass of the people. This is the soil in which the pernicious plant of fatalism, irrationalism, mysticism and superstition thrives.

Industrialists, businessmen, judges, administrators and the great majority of our politicians, with all their veneer of a "modern, western" outlook, have become the worst suppliants of astrologers and Godmen. This is understandable.

We also find endless queues of unemployed young graduates, boys and girls, our rising generations, waiting for hours in front of temples and statues just to get "*prasad* and blessing" from a priest whose only claim to education is the chanting of a few *mantras* he has learnt by rote, whose meaning he himself does not understand. These pathetic vows were not there as recently as fifteen or twenty years ago.

It would be shocking revelation for most people if someone were to conduct a study of how many of our scientists and tutors of science are scientists in the laboratory and on the campuses of universities and most pious god-worshippers and mystics in private life.

And as for our monopoly mass media, above all, the Sunday editions of our English and the Indian languages dailies, we find in them a regular flood of articles glorifying the mysteries of the ancient Indian "occult insight". Half the daily engagements appearing in our daily press are sermons on all sorts of variations of the same theme. Bharatiya Vidya Bhawan, a most prestigious institution, in fact, specialises in them. Next to sex and violence, superstition is the main theme of cinematographic films. Our television does the same, though in covert fashion.

Add to this, the systematic, nationwide propaganda of RSS journals; the esoteric orgies in the Ashrams of Godmen like late Acharya Rajneesh, the Bala Yogi, Satya Sai Baba, Mahesh Yogi and many others, and "religious" activities of barely concealed US outfits like the Krishna consciousness cult, Anand Marg and so on.

In such state of affairs, when and wherever any movement and struggle are launched by progressive and left forces against social inequalities, exploitations and oppressions etc. then the reactionaries, fascists and communalist forces start to counter these movements and struggles through religion and religious consciousness as ideological weapons. So to counter the ideological weapons of these forces, the development, the assimilation and the propagation of the scientific social consciousness, the doctrine of atheism, the philosophy of dialectical and historical materialism have become the urgent task of the day, only then we will get succeeded in secularisation of politics and so the state. Any social problem, whatever its dimension and intensity may be, is part and parcel of the basic problems and the basic problem is primarily a political problem.

Concept of Secularism

In a simple language secularism is a social doctrine, ideology and principle concerned with the separation of religion from the politics and so from the state. To give it in a concrete and material form is a very difficult task but not impossible. The doctrine of secularism is inseparable from the doctrine of socialism. So to establish the rule of secularism is the same as to establish socialism, a genuine democratic social system based on social ownership of the means of production and distribution of the material goods. The roots of secularism lie in the process of fighting against all sorts of inequalities, exploitations and oppressions. So, it is an ideology and a doctrine of the non-owning class, labouring class and exploited class. It cannot be the ideology and doctrine of owning class, leisured class and exploiting class. The doctrine of secularism helps us in defining the social groups on the basis of classes, not on the basis of religion and race.

The greatest enemy of secularism is communalism. It is also an ideology which tries to define the social groups on the basis of religion and race for the political ends. The roots of communalism lie in unequal, irrational and inhuman capitalistic path of development of the society. Communalists have nothing to do with the human sufferings and the basic problems of the society.

The reactionaries, communalists, fascists and so on, who are the worst enemies of society, invariably keep on pumping most sinister ideological concepts into the minds of the people. They consciously and systematically utilize the ideological weapons of mysticism, superstition, irrationalism, fatalism, revivalism, chauvinism, sadism, cynicism and what not to poison the minds of the people and divert their attention from the basic problems, their sufferings and struggle for social progress and social justice. Religion and religious consciousness are their main ideological weapons.

Religion and Idealism

Religion is a specific type of social consciousness. It is a superstructure. In that capacity it deals with the relation between the man and God. But the superstructure has material roots and if it were not to strengthen its material foundation, it would not survive as a superstructure. Religion is an illusive consciousness, an inverted consciousness as it gives a temporary pleasure that is not real.

The philosophical base of religion is idealism. Idealism is a philosophical doctrine which rejects the fundamental reality of matter, of nature; which rejects sense perception as valid instrument of knowledge and practice as the criterion of truth—such a philosophy necessarily leads to mysticism, agnosticism, theism, superstition and all sorts of obscuranticism. It is for this reason that idealism is basically wrong and reactionary, and it is from this standpoint that materialists reject it. It seems, in nature and in society, all objects and phenomena are isolated, independent from one another. What is more, idealism leads to a man to be ego-centric, individualistic in nature and essence, because it gives a principle of merger of one's soul into Brahm. It is pertinent to mention here the role of religion and idealism in human development in general and toiling masses in particular. In the words of S. G. Sardesai : "In the long ages of human history, the dominant role of idealism and religion has been of restricting human thought within a very narrow compass; of making humanity a victim of mysticism, superstition and ignorance; of turning illusion into reality and reality into illusion; of discouraging, if not actually persecuting the advance of science; of being a tool in the hands of the exploiting and governing classes for robbing the toiling masses and keeping them in a state of intellectual and spiritual superfaction."[1] In this context, it is also important to mention the social role of Vedanta philosophy which is absolutely idealism in its nature and essence because it has been the dominant philosophy of the Indian ruling class, owning class, leisured class and exploiting class since time immemorial. In the same book S. G. Sardesai writes : "Denial of material reality; considering physical labour as degraded; contempt and hatred for those who worked with their hands all the three were interconnected and went hand in hand with the equation of ultimate reality with pure consciousness, the pure idea, the *atma.*

This is the decisive proof that Vedanta was the ideological weapon of Brahmin and Kshatriya for riveting the chains of servitude on the feet of the toiling shudras and vaishyas. For all who have eyes to see and an impartial mind to think, this was the undeniable social role, the social function of Vedanta."[2]

However, Vedanta is still the dominant philosophy. It justifies the social division of labour-based caste, the hierarchical social order of *chaturvarnya* social formation. Vedanta and *chaturvarnya* social formation are inseparable, that means there is no Vedanta without *chaturvarnya* and there is no *chaturvarnya* without Vedanta. So, Vedanta philosophy cannot be the philosophical base for fighting against communalism.

Materialism as the Philosophical Base of Scientific Secularism

Since secularism is the doctrine and ideology concerned with the fate and destiny of the millions of toiling masses, so the most important philosophical question arises which philosophical view, theory and epistemological principle can help us in understanding the problem of secularism; in strengthening, developing and sustaining the ideology and doctrine of secularism. It is definitely materialism not idealism as we have seen above.

Materialism is a philosophical doctrine which holds that consciousness, thoughts, ideas, principles, doctrines etc. which certainly include ethical and cultural values, arise from the material conditions of social life. What it denies is the theory that they are implanted in the minds of men by supernatural, spiritual power, in a word by God. What it denies is that virtuousness results from the mandate of God. What it denies is that God showers his blessings on the virtuous and punishes the sinful. Materialism provides philosophical base to a man to be socio-centric and collectivism in outlooks and in views.

Materialism, particularly dialectical materialism has the postulates about reality that all the objects and phenomena in society are interconnected, interrelated and interconditioned; there is a unity of determinant and determined instances and there is a unity of correspondent and contradictory instances.

The basic social contradictions in class society are : between slave-owners and serfs; between the peasants and the feudal lords; between bourgeoisie and the proletariat; between the labouring class and the leisured class; between the exploiting class and the exploited class and between the rulers and the ruled. It is the dialectical materialism which has the maximum possibility to resolve these contradictions in a correct way. So it has the capacity to solve the basic problems of inequality, exploitation and oppression in class society.

Since secularism is inseparable from socialism, so to understand the problem of socialism is the same as to understand the problem of secularism. And to understand the problem of socialism we must understand the extent production process, production relations in the dominant sectors of the economy. Production relations determine all the social relations.

Secularism is not a problem of mere legislative reforms and bureaucratic measures rather it is socio-political and ideological problem. We have rich and great traditions of scientific and materialist socio-philosophical schools of thought such as Lokayat, Samkhya, Buddhism, Jainism, Nyaya, Vaisheshika, Mimansa and Yoga. The views and outlooks embodied in these philosophical schools will certainly help us in fighting for the cause of secularism and socialism.

The present has a multiplicity of future and the future is multiplicity of potential developments of the present. There are objective forces at work in the present, forces which determine a range of possibilities. But this range implies neither that certain phenomena will inevitably realize themselves nor that they will realize themselves in a certain concrete form.

Strengthening Secularism

The strengthening of the doctrine and ideology of secularism is a long-term and continuous process. It required its carriers and bearers to be partisan in nature and essence, but should not be based on narrow-minded, ignorant, bigoted. We cannot stand by secularism without attacking communalism; we cannot stand by the roots of secularism without destroying the roots of communalism; we cannot stand by the philosophical base of secularism without rejecting the philosophical base of communalism; we cannot stand by the material conditions of secularism without superseding the material conditions of communalism; we cannot stand by the politics of secularism without negating the politics of communalism. In this sense, partisanship is not only unavoidable, it is necessary. Ivory tower "objectivity" is neither objective nor non-partisan. It is inanity. This is disarming the forces of progress in the face of reaction.

REFERENCES

1. Sardesai, S. G. : Progress and Conservation in Ancient India, People's Publishing House, New Delhi, 1986, p. 145.
2. *Ibid.*, p. 116.

15

NATION-STATE, CULTURAL PLURALISM AND POWER RELATIONS

Jose Kananaikil

It has slowly begun to dawn upon us that pluralism is a reality we cannot ignore. This essay examines some aspects of this reality.

Society as Nation-State

Modern societies are complex societies. They often include diverse but interdependent subgroups sharing common boundaries and participating in the life of a nation.

Self-sufficient and homogeneous social groups with independent economic and political structures and single value systems are today hard to find if they exist at all. The original groups—races, tribes, caste systems and village communities—have become incorporated into larger wholes.

The complexity of modern societies comes not merely from the fact, that they include diverse groups and peoples. The Roman empire or the Mauryan and Gupta empires in India included diverse religious and social groups. The complexity of the new societies comes rather from the manner in which the people share in the life of the nation. Modern societies are nation-states in which individuals and groups participate in determining common boundaries and common goals, in defining common identity and in exercising the sovereignty of the nation. Here we shall consider three important aspects of modern societies : national integration, intra-national diversity and the polarization of power-relations in society.

National Integration

In modern societies, the boundaries of social groups tend to become coextensive with the legal boundaries of the nation-state. The concept of nation-state has different origin in Europe and in the post-colonial Asian and African countries. In Europe it involved the transformation of authority from patrimonial through feudal and absolutist to democratic nationalism, a process of civic incorporation through reforms of administration and services and an extension of citizenship and equality to individuals and groups. In most Asian and African countries the nation-state had its origin in the nationalist movements led by elite groups against colonial rule. After independence the nationalist movements became a search for common identity, common boundaries, common goals and the very bond of nationalism and an attempt to define rights and duties in the nation-building process.

The exercise of sovereignty, of course, differs greatly depending not only on the internal and external constraints a nation might be experiencing at a particular time, but also on the way the political elite decide to interpret its meaning. In all cases, however, whether democracies, military regimes, dictatorships or constitutional monarchies, the exercise of power is "legitimized by claims of popular mandate." Indeed, other ways of justifying authority have become inconceivable. (Bendix,1978). The national identify takes precedence over identity and attachment within the group.

Nation and Nationalism

Rupert Emerson calls nation the "terminal community," the largest community which "effectively commands men's loyalty, overriding the claims of all others, and with which, perhaps, "men most intensely and most unconditionally identify themselves" (Emerson, 1962). It has become the indispensable framework for all social, cultural, and economic activities, and is invested with "transcendent moral sanction and authority" (Young, 1976).

Nationalism thus has become a potent social force. It can give rise to an emotional bond which transcends all other bonds of group life and can inspire total commitment to the nation. Waging wars and killing people are justified when they are done in the name of the nation. Forceful occupation of territories and their people are tolerated, sometimes glorified, in the name of national security. Civil wars and movements of secession, however, are looked upon as tragic events threatening national integrity and are rarely glorified unless they succeed and begin to claim sovereignty in their own right.

In Bangladesh we have an example of secession which succeeded and in Biafra an example of one which failed. Bangladesh was received into the community of sovereign nations. Biafra, as a separate nation, was erased from the book of life.

The event of the Iranians taking the American diplomats as hostages brought contrary emotions to the Iranians and the American people. The Iranians celebrated the taking of hostages. For them it served to "humiliate" a big nation and, apparently, to strengthen internal unity. The American people were concerned not only because the life and safety of 52 people was in jeopardy, but also because what was at stake was respect for international law regarding the sovereignty of a nation. When the hostages were released, the people in the United States celebrated not only the freedom of the 52 Americans but also the freedom of the nation. During a national reception given them, President Reagan thanked them "for making us proud to be Americans."

If nationalism is to be more than an ephemeral emotionalism, it has to be based on common values. The nation usually possesses or develops a minimum of such a central value system which becomes the rallying point for national integration (Desai, 1948). In pluralistic societies, however, the central value system rarely grows into a "national culture." The zeal of the dominant groups to propagate their values as the central values, the attempt by the political elites to manufacture a national culture which suits their vision, and the fear of the minorities that the values of the dominant groups are being imposed on them, called to ambiguity, tension and conflict concerning what the nation stands for. Tamil Nadu, for example, a southern state in the Indian Union opposed what it felt was an attempt to impose Hindi, the language of the dominant northern group and their culture, on the people of the state.

It is not often recognised that the creation of a common value system in a complex society is a process which involves a continual interaction between the constituent members—social, cultural, religious and ideological groups—a process which can never be closed or the results fully defined but must always remain emergent and open-ended.

The nation also develops its own social and political institutions which attempt to subordinate the institutions of the subgroups. The national institutions allocate and distribute roles and resources, formulate social and economic policies, preserve law and order, and defined the nation from outside interference, functions the small groups can hardly fulfil (Barker, 1966).

The Process of Integration

While the emergence of the nation-state as a form of social integration is a rather recent phenomenon (it is only about two centuries old), some form of integration of individuals and social groups into political societies is as old as recorded history. Whether based on man's nature as a social being, on his desire to earn more by cooperating with others, or on his ability to exercise his power over others, some form of human organisation has always existed.

This was the case in Japan : "It was chiefly through the spread of an extended kinship system and the tightening of marriage and fictive kinship bonds with an increasingly large body of subservient family lines that the authority of the Yamato chieftain was extended (Bendix, 1978).

Earlier societies seem to have developed from extended familial and kinship ties, which gave rise to chieftains and kings, or by natural or forced accretion and assimilation of adjacent territories and their people into the core areas by trading groups, and military leaders.

Pounds and Bell (1964) examined the territorial growth of twenty-five European states and found that accretion and assimilation around a nuclear or a core area was the major process by which they came to be. The core areas themselves seem to have grown in this way.

Fustel de Coulanges (1956) refers to the difficulties experienced in earlier times in forming regular societies : "The city was a confederation of groups that had been established before it. .... We should not lose sight of regular societies. The social tie was not easy to establish between these human beings who were so diverse, so free, so inconstant."

Sometimes, they grew beyond regional kingdoms into sub-continental empires like the Mauryan and the Gupta empires in India. Integration in all these cases was as varied as being ruled by a chieftain or being a tributary to a loosely knit empire, being protected by a powerful king or being exploited by the core area and its people.

In some cases integration was the result of conquest from outside or large scale immigration. We have the latest example of foreign domination in the colonial rule. In Australia, in many states of South America, the United States and Canada, the large number of immigrant settlers built new nations for themselves. The natives were often excluded from this process, sometimes relegated to inferior peripheral areas or even exterminated.

The eme gence of the nation-state brought an altogether new principle of tegration, the principle of self-rule. This principle of self-rule wa ypically expressed by Daniel Manin of Venice of 1854. To Lord Jo Russel's suggestion that if Italians would only keep quiet, Austr would be more humane and would grant them more privileges tha they could secure by insurrection, he replied (Emerson 1962).

> We do n t ask that Austria be humane and liberal in Italy—which after all, would be impossible for her even if she desired; *we ask her to get out*. We have no concern with her humanity and her liberalism; we wish to be masters in our own house.

Manin's motto was reechoed in other places. First in Europe, then in the colonial countries, self-rule was achieved sometimes peacefully, but often with violence. The examples of France, Russia and of the United States became models to which many other nations would look up and which they would translate into their own struggle as circumstances demanded or allowed.

The self-rule meant transference of sovereignty from the king or the colonial state to the nation. The new nation-state became the absolute sovereign and representative of the people.

This principle of self-rule worked very differently for Europe and for the new nations of Asia and Africa. For, while the European nation-states had already been moulded into a certain homogeneity of culture and language, to a considerable degree such homogeneity was conspicuously absent in most of the new nation-states of Asia and Africa. Yet, it was precisely this model of homogeneity which was taken over by the political leaders of the new nation-states. According to (Emerson, 1962).

> The ideal model of the nation toward which the European precedents pointed, even though no such nation ever existed in total purity, is a single people, traditionally fixed on a well-defined territory, speaking the same language and preferably a language all its own, possessing a distinctive culture, and shaped to a common mould by many generations of shared historical experience . . . If this ideal model was peculiarly applicable to the original examples of England and France, it was not wholly a caricature of a number of other European peoples, but it was frequently far out of line for peoples outside the European orbit.

Added to this was the fact that in many cases the boundaries of these new nations were somewhat artificial in so far as they were administrative units created out of divergent social, cultural and political units by the colonial rulers.

All this, of course, does not mean that the new nations of Asia and Africa had no common identity or that they could not grow nation-states. In India, for example, in spite of its linguistic, cultural and religious diversity, an integrative process was already at work. The nationalist movement in India was preceded by intellectual, religious and social reform movements (Desai, 1948; Seal, 1969).

In fact, these religio-reform movements, the Brahmo Samaj, the Prarthana Samaj, the Arya Samaj, and others, were in different degrees, endeavours to recast old religion into a new form suited to meet the needs of the new society.

The liberal ideas from the West, the religious revival inside, and the common administrative system developed by the Mughal empire and revived by the British, shaped nationalist movement. According to Desai : "As a result of the impact of forces of Indian and world development, an increasing strata of the Indian people evolved a national consciousness and outlook and were drawn into the orbit of the nationalist movement."

Different processes were at work which in different ways brought Indians "closer to political equality, cultural homogeneity, and structural unity" (Rudolph and Rudolph, 1967).

One of the peculiar problems for the Indian society was the caste system, which in the words of Edward Shils "inhibits the growth of sensibilities which are required for the perception of the moral quality of other human beings..." (Shils, 1961). But even here great transformations were taking place. Rudolph and Rudolph analysing the caste communities found:

> "their entry into extra local, social and political systems, their internal culture and structure, and their strategy have been affected by the declining hold of ritual rank on social standing as twice-born norms and symbols have become at once more accessible and less relevant; by the receding cultural influence of a once dominant and now distant Western imperial power; and by the growing influence on the definition and distribution of honour and authority and on the allocation of resources of wider access to political power, an emergent industrial and bureaucratic economy egalitarian and secular ideology and law.

An integrative process was thus already present in India at the time of independence. The important point, however, is that it was a process very different from the hypothesized and idealized process attributed by many (ex-colonials) to European nationalism. A different assumption than that of homogeneity was need for India.

At the time of independence, the elite which took charge of the national affairs had immense tasks before them : unifying the various layers of national units, allocating roles and resources, formulating laws, rebuilding economic structures and establishing a viable political authority at the centre. These tasks were made more difficult by the extreme economic and social disparities which existed between groups, and psychological incompatibility experienced by others due to separate religious and cultural existences they had lived.

As the task of national integration began to unfold in India, some of the unsolved tensions and conflicts too began to appear. The diversity between the Hindus and the Muslims was too deep to be healed, and their mobilisation too strong to be subdued. This gave rise to the formation of Pakistan. The rest of the political and socio-cultural groups accepted or were made to accept the framework of the nation-state and the authority of the state represented by the political elite. A national "culture" was taken for granted or was believed to be in the making, being mainly the responsibility of the national leaders. However, it began to become clear very soon that the creation of a national culture or national identity was not merely the job of the national leaders. The dynamic interplay of the socio-cultural groups, and their role in the nation-building process began to be evident.

The question of Hindi as the national language, linguistic state boundaries, and the identity of the tribal people are some of the problems which still defy peaceful solutions.

Social integration thus seems to have entered a new stage. While some form of integration might be a human need "basic to our being" integration of individuals and groups in a nation-state has today become a social necessity.

The Russian intervention in Afghanistan, the Russian "right" to intervene in Poland, to mention only two examples, show how precarious the sovereignty of the nation-states is in the modern world and already point to a different level of sovereignty: the sovereignty of the super-powers. However, one can hardly speak of a progress or teleology in this process. On the one hand, the integration of individuals and groups into larger wholes has helped to remove the narrow confines of group life and to enhance the range of choices and possibilities for the individual in a wider society. On the other hand, a deep realisation of man in modern society has been a sense of his "loss of community" (Nisbet, 1969). The rise of the nation-states has introduced a new problem, the problem of developing a national identity without destroying group identity.

Cultural Pluralism

As there has been a movement towards integration into larger societies, there has also been a strong persistence of group-identity.

Towards the end of the last century, social scientists became increasingly concerned about what they saw as the growing anonymity in the expanding societies around them. George Simmely described this phenomenon as expanding concentric and intersecting circles into which individuals and social groups move in modern societies. As they move into wider circles, individuals become free from the constraints of their primary groups and enter into wider arenas of choices and possibilities. However, they also acquire in the process qualities of anonymity and indifference more suited to city life.

Tonnies (1957) saw in this process a definite movement away from the intimacy and the community which prevailed in earlier societies (*Gemeinschaft*) into an amorphous mass society (*Gesellschaft*), Durkheim (1964) called them "mechanical" and "organic" forms of society. (Weber, 1959) predicted the possibility of individuals being reduced to cogs in a rational, bureaucratic machine, as Hegel had predicted earlier.

These fears, fortunately, did not fully materialise. Developments in modern societies have brought about structural changes in old social groups by incorporating them into larger societies. The behavioural patterns of people have been changed by their introduction into rational and achievement-oriented modern bureaucracies in spite of these various developments, modern societies have not become anonymous mass societies. Studies on modern societies indicate that ethnic groups and caste systems still exist and that they can sometimes play important roles in giving new forms and new directions to the strivings of the people.

Rodolph and Rodolph (1967) show the constructive role caste can play in political mobilisation in India. Ethnic revivalism can be seen even in some of the more stable European states. Hechter (1977) examines the re-emergence of the Celtic regions in the United Kingdom.

While old group identities have, in some form or another, persisted in modern societies, new ones have also emerged: migrated ethnic and cultural groups, religious sects, political parties, clubs, union, and corporations. All these not only exist as stratified social groups on the basis of occupation and prestige, but also tend to become politically mobilized with varying degree of bargaining power to influence the value orientations and policy decisions at the centre.

This persistence of subcultures and substructures have generally been characterised both by statesmen of old kingdoms and by leaders of new nations as harmful to national integration. Wherever possible, they have tried to eliminate such tendencies. The leaders of new nations have generally espoused the theory of radical individualism and universalism embedded in the liberal thought and the scientific culture of the 19th and 20th centuries, namely, that as the objective forces of modernisation spread through society, subcultures and substructures would disappear, giving way to an enhancement of individual freedom and homogeneous culture.

While earlier social thinkers like Durkheim, Tonnies and Simmel spoke of the anomie, and impersonality of the mass culture, the modern political thinkers envisaged a nation-state with a homogeneous culture and individual freedom.

These expectations, however, remain unrealised. Even in the American "melting pot," where this theory had the best chance for success, the forces of modernisation—a political culture, relatively homogeneous class structure, national mass media, and residential mobility—have not neutralised the power of ethnic or religious bonds or of ideological and interest oriented polarisations within the nation (Rudolph and Rudolph, 1967).

Without some group association, it is difficult for individuals to survive. The society around them has become so large and so complex, the bureaucracy so impersonal, that no individual today can defend his rights by himself. Moreover, for most people individual fulfilment would seem to require that values and motivations are brought within the reach of one's everyday life and are concretised within realisable emotional bonds. The sense of belonging to a voluntary association seems to fulfil these needs.

These reflections seem to suggest that a society which is based upon the principles of radical individualism and homogeneity of culture may not be the best kind of society. A de Tocqueville, 1969). They further suggest that individual freedom and growth is enhanced, rather than smothered, by voluntary group associations. Genuine social integration, then, it would seem, requires that the identity and freedom of voluntary associations and para communities are not excluded.

Centre and Periphery

I am indebted to Edward Shils (1975) for these concepts, however, as indicated in the text, these terms are here used in a somewhat different sense.

What is characteristic of modern societies is not merely that they consist of stratified social groups. The increasing self-awareness and self-mobilisation among these groups have tended to make them subsystems within the nation with varying degree of power to influence the central system. Challenges and demands from these subsystems can give rise to various forms of conflict: ethnic (south Africa, the United States, Canada and Belgium), caste based (India), religious (Northern Ireland), ideological (Italy and every nation in which there are organised political parties), and economic (Latin America). The encounters and interactions between these subsystems also tend to become polarised. One important polarisation that can be seen in modern societies, especially in the new nations of the third world, is the polarisation of social groups into the centre and the periphery.

The concepts of centre and periphery can be understood in at least three different senses. They can be taken in a geographical sense to refer to a central or core area and its surrounding peripheral regions. As has been mentioned earlier, most European nation-states seem to have developed through a process of a central or core area extending its influence over the peripheral regions.

The power exercised by the core region over the peripheral regions has sometimes been called "internal colonialism (Hechter 1977).

Extending the colonial situation in which societies where subjected to racially and culturally different people from outside, internal colonialism refers to the domination and exploitation of the peripheral hinterlands by the central regions of the same society or continent.

Edward Shils (1975) uses these terms to refer to the cultural system of a society. The centre here means the central value system of a nation, while the periphery refers to the masses who are not fully integrated into the central value system. The modern societies are characterised, according to Shils, by the increasing demand by the masses to be included in the central value system and in the central institutions.

The concepts of centre and periphery can also be used in a political sense (Gerald A Heeger 1974). Here the centre refers to the national elite and their followers who control the political power and the policy and decision making processes in the nation. They control the government, the bureaucratic machinery, the party caucuses, the news media and other forces of power in the nation. The centre may be headed by a charismatic leader who is supported by an elite group or it may consist of a loosely knit alliance of elites who control the political institutions of the nation. The periphery, then, in a democratic country can be conceived as those local leaders and their followers who for various reasons play little or insignificant roles in the political system of the nation.

The periphery is, therefore, different from the opposition party or parties. While not directly controlling the political machinery in the country, the opposition parties may have considerable resources at their disposal and can sometimes challenge the ruling party. In contrast, the peripheral groups are unorganised and with little or no resources. They are sometimes patronised by the ruling party or the opposition parties as the case may be, but are often exploited rather than benefit from such dealings. They have practically no control over the decision-making process in the country, and their meagre resources usually would be exploited by interested parties. Any concentration of power at the periphery would be treated as a threat both by the ruling party and by the opposition party or parties, and would be opposed.

In this essay we have used the terms centre and periphery both in a cultural and in a political sense. In modern societies political power seems to be the decisive factor which determines a group's role in the national life. However, in India, the centre and periphery seem to be drawn also on distinct cultural or caste lines. By the centre, then, we mean those social or caste groups in India who control the economic resources and the political institutions of the nation. By the periphery we mean those social groups who, due to their meagre economic and political resources, are unable to compete with other groups or to demand their just share in the nation-building process and are often exploited.

It is argued that in spite of the widespread poverty and linguistic, cultural and regional diversity in India, it is possible to detect a polarisation of social groups into centre and periphery that certain caste groups, a minority in themselves, who are called the "upper castes," control most of the economic resources of the nation, form the dominant culture, and constitute the political centre, while others remain socially and economically at the bottom and are often exploited by the rest. It is further suggested that after more than fifty years of independence, generous constitutional provisions to protect the peripheral groups, attempts of liberal social reforms both by the government and by social reformers, this process of polarisation does not seem to have been reversed.

Who, then, constitute the centre in Indian society, and who the periphery ? How do centre and periphery come into being ? How do they interact ? How do they affect social and national integration in India ?

Anyone who looks at the Indian political scene can see that India is an arena of power politics which is based on a power relations between social groups. Those who once controlled power and hence controlled other social groups are realizing that power is slipping away from their hands. Those who were oppressed and marginalised hitherto are beginning to wake up and to ask for their place in society. Some win in the process, some lose, still others are being wiped out in the process. Those who would like to live are beginning to realise that it is not enough to live and let live. One has, both as an individual and as a member of a community, actively involve oneself in what is going on around and form alliances with those who think alike, and take a stand against oppression and injustice and try to make the world one lives in a better place to live not only for oneself but also for others.

NOTES

Barker, Ernest. (1944) 1966. *The Development of Public Services in Western Europe 1660-1930*. Hamden, Connecticut : Archor Books.

Bendix, Reinhard. [(1964, 1967) 1977]. *Nation-Building and Citizenship : Studies of One Changing Social Order*. New Enlarged Edition. Berkeley : University of California Press.

Desai, A. R. 1948. *Social Background of Indian Nationalism.* Bombay : Oxford University Press.

Durkheim, Emile. 1964. *The Division of Labour in Society.* Translated by George Simpson. New York : Free Press of Glencoe.

Emerson, Rupert. (1962). *From Empire to Nation : The Rise to Self-Assertion of Asian and African Peoples.* Cambridge, Massachusetts : Harvard University Press.

Fustel de Coulanges, Numa Denis. (1864) 1956. *The Ancient City : A Study on the Religion, Laws and Institutions of Greece and Rome.* Translated by Willard Small, Garden City, New York : Doubleday, Anchor.

Heeger, Gerald A. 1974. *The Politics of Underdevelopment*, New York : St. Martin's Press.

Nisbet, Robert A. (1953) 1969. *The Quest for Community.* Oxford : Oxford University Press.

Pounds, N. J. G. and, Bell, S. 1964, "Core Areas and the Development of the European State System. " *Annals of the American Association of Geographers* 54(1) : 240-40.

Rudolph, Lloyd I., and Rudolph, 1967. *The Modernity of Tradition : Political Development in India.* Chicago : University of Chicago Press.

Seal, Anil. 1968. *The Emergence of Indian Nationalism : Competition and Collaboration in the Later Nineteenth Century.* Cambridge : At the University Press.

Shils, Edward. 1975. *Centre and Periphery : Essays in Macrosociology.* Selected Papers of Edward Shils, Vol. 2. Chicago : University of Chicago Press.

Tonnies, Ferdinand. 1957. *Community and Society* (Gemeinschaft and Gesellschaft). Translated by Charles P. Loomis. East Lansing : Michigan State University Press.

Young, Crawford. 1976. *The Politics of Cultural Pluralism.* Madison, Wisconsin : The University of Wisconsin Press.

16

SAMAVAYA EVA SADHU

B. P. Sinha

The question of national integration is staring in the face of knowledgeable Indians. The question is why in India this problem is uppermost in mind. In England, the Scots, the Irish and the Anglo-Saxons have linguistic differences, even ethnic complexes and off and on separatist voices are raised in Scotland and Wales at least. But the fear of dismemberment of England is not seriously apprehended. But why in India ? The reasons lie in the long political history, geographical barriers, and cultural or sub-cultural identities. We have more than 16 officially recognised languages and many more knocking for admission. There are inaccessible mountainous areas with which majority of plains people have little contact. Political history of India for most of its recorded account is regional history, of regional conflicts. Before the British politically united India by middle of the 19th century (Punjab was annexed in 1848), there were the Nanda-Maurya age (400-180 B.C.), the Gupta period (350-550 A.D.), the Turco-Afghan period (1300-1450), the Mughal period (1556-1707 A.D.) —the short periods of reasonable and varying degree of political unification in the context of much longer spells of political disunity and regional conflicts from the point of view of national unity and integration. India is not a land of many races only, it is a land of many languages, many religions and many cultures, often insisting on separate identities, and not amenable to merger with one another by persuasion, propaganda or by force.

So there were and there continue to be many hurdles for national integration and political unity. The British first time after the Mauryan experiment imposed political unity, administrative uniformity and for administrative purposes reduced the linguistic jungle into manageable problem by encouraging English and Persian in the early period of British administration, and elites including the administrator class were encouraged or rather induced to accept in the earlier period Sanskrit or Prakrit, English or Urdu and Hindustani latter. So a sense of political oneness was made to prevail, but it was hardly a meeting of hearts and minds. It was the national movement led by Mahatma Gandhi which provided the emotional base for national unity. Not only for common aspiration for political freedom but the vehicle for its all-India articulation was simple Hindi or Urdu termed by Gandhiji as Hindustani. All leaders of different linguistic areas tried even in broken accent to speak in Hindustani in regions which was Hindi-dominated area. And the strength of nationalist forces for political freedom and national integration was tested when the British attempted to Balkanize India (after partition) by giving freedom to the erstwhile hundreds of states to choose their future. It was not only the vision and iron-handedness of that Iron Man—Sardar Patel but the wave of nationalism which was sweeping the people of the native states and also in most of the rulers, that enabled independent India to face the worst crisis on the morrow of independence to preserve the unity of India as it stood after the creation of Pakistan. That nationalism and commitment to the unity of country is not skin deep, but is deeply ingrained in our consciousness has been proved more than once when the country faced foreign aggressions. The whole country, not withstanding diversity in religion, language, culture, and race stood as a solid rock.

But spirit of nationalism and concern for territorial unity of the country should not find expression only in the wake of emergencies. It should become a part and parcel of our day-to-day lives with our neighbours, with members of different communities, of different linguistic groups, of different socio-economic level, And that is the rule.

Here our history may help us in charting our politics and course of action. From the earliest periods of our known history—Indus Valley Civilization we have been faced with the problem of many races and religions. In the development of the Harappan culture different races—Proto-Australoid, Mediterranean, Alpinoid and the Mongoloid—all principal races of men contributed. The chronological evidence speaks not only of the diverse racial elements, but also of free racial mixture. Until the Harappan script is deciphered to the satisfaction of all knowledgeable scholars, we will never be able to even guess the distinct contribution of the different human groups of the consolidation of the civilisation. But the material remains of the culture as a whole suggest considerable unity in the vast area under it (larger than Mesopotamia) and that also for nearly 800 years. Some have explained this general uniformity to be a product of centralised imperialism controlling the entire area. But one should not over-emphasize the general uniformity. There are significant regional variations. We do not find the popular mother-goddess figurines and the linga-yoni stones in Kalibanga, and the Surkotda fortification and layout have some distinguishing features, we have nothing of the water-tank of Mohenjodaro in any other city but we have brick platform with hints of sacrificial ritual in Kalibanga which is not met with in any other excavated Harappan sites. What is to say is that in the context of general uniformity in architecture and cultural traits, there were regional variations which enriched the overall cultural complex. Even in the same city seals and other remains show a variety of religious beliefs and practices such as mother-goddess worship, animal worship, linga worship, sacrifices of animal or even human, tree worship, worship of unnatural and composite animals, Pasupati and Yoga and of tirtha etc.

It is quite difficult to believe that one religious system enveloped all these diverse traits. Different religions with different modes of worship must have prevailed—both primitive like tree worship and highly developed as Yoga. Some of the seals show a combination of different religious motifs and this may suggest syncreticism in vogue even at that time. What we wish here to emphasize is that even in this early period of Indian history we find evidence of diverse religious systems not only co-existing but even trying to arrive at some synthesis. This picture vaguely seen in the Indus Valley is more or less repeated later in our long history. A propensity to co-exist with diverse elements and an attempt to synthesize them into an acceptable form appear to be some of the most important plus-points of Indian history through the ages. Now this characteristic of Indian cultural history can be seen at work in social, political and art traditions, but here we are concerned with the religious traditions contributing to a working synthesis and promoting coexistence of different sects and different philosophies.

In the Vedic period we come across quite early two antagonistic communities—the Arya and the Dasa, and the *Rgveda* is replete with references to their wars and their contempt for and hostility with which the Aryans speak of their language and culture. But even among the Aryan groups as well there are references of conflicts, references to rival families of priesthoods (Vasistha and Visvamitra) and it is not unlikely that this rivalry, basically political, made some to make the *dasyas* or the *asuras* their allies. This could, in course of time, create conditions for the mutual give and take, for co-existence between the Aryans and the non-Aryans. This should be most visible in the social and religious fields; the Vratyas and their gods appear to have been grudgingly accepted into the Aryan fold. A comparative study of the *Rgveda* and *Atharvaveda* shows that the latter contains traditions and beliefs of communities which were not earlier shared by the *Rgvedic* people, but these have been accepted in the Vedic system. The *Vedic mantras* give us a large number of gods and some goddesses, and it appears that there was sometimes some sort of competitiveness, rivalry between votaries of different gods which may have caused some tension in the community as a whole. Instead of letting this grow as a cancerous growth to dismember the social polity and religious poise, the sages emphasized the futility, rather absurdity of claims or counterclaims about the superiority of this or that god favourite of one or other Aryan community, as all the gods of all the groups and communities, even of non-Aryans or just admitted non-Aryans with their religious system into the Aryan fold, are the reflections of one and the same supreme, the only truth "Ekam sad vpra bahoda badanti". Truth is one but sages call it by many names. This great wisdom proclaiming the unity of all religions, the belief in the Ultimate Reality which is one and one only, was uttered in the time of the *Rgveda*. It is not a call for confrontation, it does not say that our God is the one and all the other gods being worshipped by different groups of people are false. It says all gods are true as they are reflections of the same Ultimate Reality, are religious and sectarian conflict for success of one god over the other is meaningless. This is the wise message which has to be repeated again and again. It is the key to the resolution of religious disharmony and discord, and indubitably suggests that all religions so far as they are espoused as instruments to reach the Ultimate God can and should co-exist, and the votaries of one need not, must not attack the god or religion of the others, as his god and gods of others are all identical with the Supreme God. The message in short is *Samavaya eva Sadhu* : Religious Concord is good.

In the later Vedic down to the Upanishadic period we find that there was not only considerable socio-economic change but also in the religious and philosophical fields diverse voices were heard. The Brahmanas and the Kshatriyas had cemented their unholy alliance so to say to assure their privileged position, social eminence, and political authority over the common people constituting the two classes—the Vaisyas and the Sudras, the lowest in the Varna-order solidified by the priests on religious dispensation claiming divine sanction. The innocent-looking *Varna vyavastha* based on reasonable division of labour had, by this time, been transformed into a fundamental divinely determined hierarchical social polity with permanently assigned duties and privileges to the four classes, on the basis of birth. Social mobility up and down this vertical ladder was disfavoured. The Brahmanas pledged support to the king who from now depended more on their support and on the sacrifices prescribed by them for stability and growth than on the elected *samitis* and powerful *sabhas* which now when existed remained only a king's court. The king in his turn assured even out of turn protection to the Brahmanas, their position and self, and contributed to their material well-being by abundance of gifts (*dana, dakshina*), most of which were obtained from the *Vis*, the common people who were regarded as only for being eaten by the two upper Varnas. The sacrifices were often accompanied with lot of violence in the shape of loss of life of various animals to propitiate the deities to help and promote the interests of the king, the performer of the sacrifices. The sacrifices, numerous and tedious as well as time-consuming, had almost reduced religion to a set of rituals and pursuit of the Reality and quest for spiritual values had been cornered to take back seats.

But dissent was not far away. Towards the end of the period, 1000 B.C.—800 B.C., iron had come into use. This had made clearance of jungle and preparation of land fit for cultivation easier, and so large landholdings came into being, and the Vaisyas and the Sudras took the leading part which required constant working by hand disfavoured by the two upper castes. Naturally this new class of hardworking landholders was desirous of getting its due place under the sun. They were in need of more and more draught animals (oxen and buffaloes) for agricultural purposes and their loss in the Brahmanic sacrifices was not palatable to this class. Moreover, workers in metals—copper, bronze and iron—were being grouped into distinct professional classes becoming more and more useful to households, agriculturists and military personnel. Their social status being low in Brahmanic order was not in consonance with their growing utility and even economic health. And then there were even among the two upper classes a large number of persons as teachers, students, *parivrajakas* and *sanyasis*, and even some kings (Jawali) and their sons who were disgusted with the ritual-ridden animal sacrifice promoting religious order. These people began to question the validity of the sacrifices or the loss of animal-lives. This was the background in which the muted expression of dissent against the then prevailing socio-religious orders based on inherent adherence to the principle of inequality of man is seen in the Upanishadic literature proclaiming *ahimsa permo dharmah* and giving more importance to the realization of Reality than to material and political gains and for this meditation, unflinching rational exercise was more efficacious than animal sacrifices. Now this was a clear revolt against the powers that be but there is no evidence that this was confronted with measures of repression of any kind. The Brahmanic order in self-defence realising the loss of clientele among the intellectuals and some enlightened Kshatriyas tried to strengthen their hold over the common people by formulating a scheme of numerous *samskaras* which the people had to perform for their interest—material and spiritual. The Grahya, the Kalpa and Srauta Sutras were the text-books for the observance of the *samskaras* under the guidance of priests, and to impress on the royalty as well as the common people their bounden duty to follow and protect the Varnasrama order that the Dharmasutras were composed.

Notwithstanding these defensive measures the dissidents continued to grow in numbers and importance, and Buddhism, Jainism and Ajivikism to name the prominent protestant movements, became popular. These not only ignored the Brahmanical sacrifices but rejected totally its rationale and value and while it is to be conceded that even the Buddha did not reject the Varna order all round which had by then become a part of life of the people, he challenged the Brahmanical thesis of birth as the basis of the fourfold division. Buddha's clarion call '*jatima puccha, kamma puccha*' was a clear denunciation of the Brahmanical value system. Growing emphasis on a life of recluse was certainly a concomitant factor in the wake of the movements, and this disdain of material world for peace in the next or liberation from worldly life had a reaction in the Carvaka philosophy which believed in fully enjoying the world by all means.

It can never be overemphasised that again the hundred flowers blossomed. Very differing and contradictory philosophies were being aired and different religions were coming up. Besides the intransigent status-quo fundamentalist Brahmanical learned priesthood believing in sacrifices and *samskaras*, there were world-denying Vedantists, the Middle-Patha preaching Buddhists, the believer in austerities and no-karma Jains, the fanatically non-believing Ajivikas, and pleasure-seeking Carvakas, all these were preaching and propagating their views, holding animated discussions, criticising bitterly rival-thoughts and creeds, with practically no bolts barred. It appears that the Buddha and Mahavira were at the same place and holding parallel sabhas but they are never reported to have met. The Ajivikas were very bitter against the Jains and *vice-versa*, and the hostility between the Brahmins and the Jains is well known. There was no love lost between the Buddhists and the Brahmins, and there were philosophical contests between them trying to nullify each other's value system, and Sankaracarya—the best exponent of Vedanta was a crusader against Buddhist philosophy. But in spite of bitter controversies, expressions of ridicule by one against the others, there is no indubitable evidence of curtailment of freedom of expression, no instance of disturbing the sabha of one by the followers of other sects, under kings devoted to one religion or another, to one teacher or the other. Even kings changed their religions or teachers, but it did not mean the religious persecution of others. In Indian history there has been hardly a Henry VIII, Edward or Mary of England or Philip of Spain. There was no inquisition.

The Mauryan age which in many ways forms the most creative period in ancient Indian history, saw the socio-religious conflicts in correct perspective and offered solutions which have not lost their relevance today. Megasthenes found the Saivas and Vaisnavas quite popular. Their religious processions have been seen by him. Kautilya mentions many Vedic and Brahmanic deities like Indra, Brahma, Varuna, Yama, Siva, Vaishravana, Asvins, Senapati, Apratihata (Vishnu). But he also refers to some other deities and demons who were propitiated by *mantras* and had magical power to cure diseases and remove dangers. In this list mention is made of Bali, Sambara, Vairocana, Maraka, Kumbh etc. some of which we identify as Vedic Asuras fighting the devas. Some saints like Galava, Sravani, Narada, Devala besides Krishna and Kansa are also deified. Naga-Pratima also is referred to. So we here find different kinds of divinities probably worshipped by different layers of the community. Kautilya refers to such Brahmanical sacrifices as Asvamedha, Maha Kacchavarchana, Agnistoma, Somavikraya, Brihaspatisvama etc. which must have entailed animal or even human sacrifices. Superstitions and faith in *mantra-tantra* and magic to ward off trouble and performance of various ceremonies for material comfort and goods were quite common among people and it appears from Kautilya that the state believed in these and encouraged these. He mentions ascetics living in asramas and pashandas, and a league of the pashandas (pashanda samcha), Buddhists and Ajivikas are mentioned. The Jains or Nirganthas are not explicitly referred to. Kautilya has very clear preference for the Brahmanical religion, and the varnashrama dharma. He clearly shows his dislike of wandering ascetics who were not Vanaprasthis or Sanyasis in accordance with the Brahmanical order, and he would like to keep these wandering young ascetics (men and women) in new villages which the state has set up, as he thinks they would disturb or corrupt the simple village folk from productive activities by encouraging ascetism and wandering. Candragupta Maurya may have become Jain in later years but Jainism by that time was not a formidable religion. But during the last years of the first Maurya's reign and certainly by the time of Asoka's rule, Jains or Nirganthas must have gained some ground, as Asoka's inscription (P. E . VII) mentions them as coming in the purview of the Dharmamahamatras care. So the picture that emerges is a scene of plurality of religious systems and the state trying to put restrictions on free movement of ascetics who must have been mostly of heretical (non-Brahmanical) sects.

So the religious scene was not that placid, and due to religious ferment with the consequential social unrest continuing for some centuries, a conscientious ruler and a true humanitarian as Asoka was not slow to see the erosion in the traditional, social and religious values. He says : "In times past for many hundreds of years there had ever been promoted the killing of animals and the hurting of living beings, discourtesy for relatives (Jatish), and discourtesy to Brahmanas and Sramanas (R. E. IV)." Asoka, the rationalist, disfavoured people particularly women having superstitious beliefs and performing many ceremonies (*mangalas*) to ensure safe journey, to cure illness, or at the marriage of a son or a daughter, and some of which in his opinion were vulgar and useless (R. E. IX). And we have already seen that on non-Brahmanical ascetics some restrictions of movement were placed earlier (Kautilya), which Asoka did not relish. Asoka had been converted to Buddhism and he did many things to promote the spread of Buddhism, particularly by raising stupas and endowing Buddhist monks with money and land. A late Buddhist work informs us that his overgenerosity to the Buddhists had caused opposition to his policy by a group of officers led by his amatya Radhagupta. There may be not much truth in the legend contained in Asokavadana, but Asoka's liberalism to Buddhist Samgha cannot be disputed. That this may have raised eyebrows among the other contemporary religious sects is quite natural. Asoka could not have been unaware of this religious tension. This may have further induced or provoked the votaries of other sects, and in some such assemblies some may have praised their own sects and disparaged sects other than their own. Free religious preaching and propaganda, rival or competitive assemblies being addressed by sect-leaders was a common phenomenon at least since the later Vedic period and which got momentum in the days of the Buddha and thereafter. In such assemblies when some adherents of other religions may have been present, denunciation of rival religions and even resort to loose tongue without reasonable restraint on one's observation at public places or at public gatherings could have contributed to the increasing intensity of tension gripping the communities as a whole. It is possible that at the back of the heightened tense situation was the actual economic damage to the Brahmanas from banning of animal sacrifices and condemning of various mangalas which contributed to the swelling of the Brahmanas' pockets. The position of the Brahmanas was probably further undermined when the influence of Brahmana as *purohit* in administration was reduced. Socio-religious tension is a complex matter, and in one form or the other economics affects it more or less.

Asoka besides being a humanist and pious person by himself was also the emperor of all-India wherein lived hundreds and thousands of ardent devoted men and women influenced by their respective religious leaders. The socio-religious tension could assume dangerous dimension; it was not only peace that was threatened, the whole fabric of political unity, social stability was at stake. Asoka had consciously adopted the policy of making Dharma a part of people's life not for disintegration but for integration of varied communities of diverse social and religious orders.

And so Asoka decided to diffuse the tension, which to him was unwarranted and to make clear to all that though he was a Buddhist, he entertained only good for all religions irrespective of a particular religion one or other of his subjects followed. He could very well have adopted the short-sighted policy of using Buddhism as a check on increasing Brahmana power, but Buddhism was never effectively used as an anti-Brahmanical weapon (Romila Thapar, Asoka and the Decline of the Mauryan Empire, paperback edition, p. 57). The Asokan states's policy of treating all religious groups Brahmanas and Sramanas equal is attested to by his edicts which proclaim the emperor's liberalism and respect to Brahmanas and Sramanas alike (R. E. III, IV, IX and X). He excavated at least two rock-cut caves in Barabar Nagarjuni hills for the Ajivikas whose hostility to Buddhism was well known. Government officers were made to busy themselves in the promotion of the welfare of the Brahmanas, Ajivikas and the Nirganthas (Jains) (P.E. VII). But he was now more concerned about the interrelations between the different sects and to emphasize value of co-existence in the interest of even the augmentation of their respective faiths. R. E. XII constitutes a landmark in the long history of religions in India and is almost a blueprint of the religious policy of a state confronted with religious pluralism. Asoka realised that the greatest risk to communal peace lies in unrestrained use of speech. One cannot improve on what Asoka says—"The Beloved of the Gods, the King Priyadarsi, honours all sects and both ascetics and laymen, with gifts and various forms of recognition. But the Beloved of the Gods does not consider gifts or honour to be as important as the advancement of the essential doctrines of all sects. This progress of the essential doctrines takes many forms, but its basis is the control of one's speech so as not to extol one's own sect or disparage another's on unsuitable occasions, or at least to do so only mildly on certain occasions. On each occasion one should honour another man's sect, for by doing so one increase the influence of one's own sect and benefits that of the other man while by doing otherwise one diminishes the influence of one's own sect and harms the other man's. Again whosoever honours his own sect and disparages that of another man, wholly out of devotion to his own, with a view to showing it in a favourable light, harms his own sect even more seriously. Therefore, concord is to be commended (Samavayo eva Sadhu) (Gir VI), so that men may hear one another's principles and obey theirs. This is the desire of the Beloved of the gods, that all sects should be well informed and should teach that which is good, and that everywhere their adherents should be told, "the Beloved of the gods does not consider gifts or honour to be as important as the progress of the essential doctrines of all sects (*Saravadhi*). Many are concerned with this matter—the officers of the Dhamma, the women's officers, the managers of the state farms, and other classes of officers (dhamma mahamata ca ithijhakha-mahamata-ca vacha-bhumika (*cowpens*) ca ane ca nikaya)".

This long extract's relevance in today's India is self evident, and the prescriptions for the removal or containment of the malignancy in the form of religious feuds or communal tension should be as efficacious as in the time of Asoka, who announced "that this is the fruit of it, viz. the increased influence of one's own sect and glory to Dhamma".

Asoka realised that communal peace was essential for the success of his policy of the conquest of Dhamma, and he found the former in real danger notwithstanding his proclaimed policy of treating all religious communities equally in so far as gifts and occasions of honour to them were concerned—liberality and honour to all Brahmanas, Sramanas, Ajivikas, Buddhists, Jains and others was observed in letter and spirit. It underlies that fact that neutral role of the state, or even distribution of favours equally to all religious communities is not enough to assure communal peace and tension-free society and polity. A realisation which our present leaders should note.

So long as in separate sectarian or communal gatherings speeches exhorting the comparative values of the religion : of the community vis-a-vis other religions would continue tension and fear of public expressions of competitive claims and counterclaims would persist. Asoka was not only interested in diffusing the tension but in taking away the ground under it. He did not ban such assemblies, nor he forbade speech-making, which could only for a time put the trouble under the carpet to appear soon after in serious proportions. His directions were : (i) In no gathering where one religion is being extolled, other religions should never be spoken ill of; (ii) in speeches exhorting the faithfuls to promote their particular sect, there should be restrictions on speech; (iii) inter-communal assemblies be held so that votaries of one religion would know and understand the principles of other religions besides their own; and (iv) this would make them realise the futility of praising one's own religion and disparaging others; (v) and this make them understand that essentials (*sara*) of all religions including his own are the same; (vi) and consequently the realisation would come that disparaging other sects with a view to enhance the value of his own sect would actually harm his religion, while praising and honouring other sects would promote the interests of his own religion. And thereby would grow among all different communities *samabhava,* a sense of equality towards all religions. And this was possible by the instrumentality or mechanism of *samavaya,* mutual meeting together (Congress of Religions), one such Vivekananda addressed in the U.S.A. long ago.

But Asoka was not satisfied by his exhortations alone, by his pronouncement of policy. His was the government that worked. He was keen on implementation of his policy by the people and by the government both. It is reasonable to believe that after this clear announcement decrying by anyone of other religions, those who defied this must have been punished. But Asoka was more interested in persuasion and in creating suitable environment. He had made it clear to both the people and the officers that promotion of essentials of religions was uppermost in his mind and head. He, therefore, wanted the Dharmamahamatras, who worked also among the Brahmanas and the Sramanas, who were looking after women and officers in charge of farms including dairy farms where people of all creeds would congregate for their needs, that they (the officers) should preach and see that *Sara* of religions is promoted. Special attention to women is to be noted; they could if properly motivated exert a moderating influence on the differing communal groups.

Asoka as we have seen claims success of his policy of increasing Dhamma which included promotion of *samabhava,* among communities. His message had to be and is to be repeated frequently as the Indian scene characterised by plurality of diverse but active religions has to be reminded again and again of the fact of pluralism and the way to overcome the problem arising out of it.

The same idea that the essentials of the religions are the same and that all gods of different cults are actually the same—Ultimate Reality is expressed by Lord Krishna in the *Bhagavad-Gita* supposed to be the Bible of Vaishnavism. He clearly says whoever worships whichever God is helped by me on his way to realise his god and to obtain desired gains (VII. 21). He further clearly says that whoever with faith and devotion worship other gods actually worship me. The *samabhava* towards all with no malice to anyone, no partiality for anyone is expressed in words of the Lord.

"All forms are directing their steps towards the own God though along the different paths"—S. Radhakrishnan. This religious electism is seen even in foreign rulers rapidly Indianised. We find on Kushana coins Iranian, Greek, Roman, Buddha and Brahmanical gods of different sub-cults. Kadphises II appears to be a Saiva; Kanishka I a Buddhist; and Vasudeva I, Vaishnava. The most-devoted Vaishnava Gupta kings established the Nalanda Mahavihara and got installed in their time linga, matrikas, Vishnu and other images in their empire and dominions, and performed vedic sacrifices such as Asvamedha. The general atmosphere of religious concord—*samavaya* is best illustrated by the existence of remains of a large Brahmanical temple dedicated probably to the Sun God in the midst of the great

Buddhist complex Nalanda Mahavihara (Stone Temple Site No. 2). Harsha, a parama-mahesvara (Devotee of Siva), was a great patron of Buddhism. Both Fah-sien and Hsuan-Tsang refer to Buddhist and Deve establishments in same localities. It may, therefore, be asserted without hesitation that generally in ancient India religious accord (*Samabhava*), and peaceful contacts (*Samavaya*) and communal peace prevailed. There were certain aberrations in the past also. Even if we leave out Buddhist stories about Pushyamitra's persecution of the Buddhists and announcement of reward of 100 dinaras for every Buddhist monk's head in Sakale, there is no doubt about Sasanka's anti-Buddhist activities.

It may be argued as I have done (Decline of the Kingdom of Magadha, pp. 105, 260-61) that his anti-Buddhist activities in Magadha may be due to political reasons. We know that competition between rival philosophies and desire of one religion to score over the other, surfaced rather as uncomonly sometimes. We have in the Buddhist iconography and some Buddhist icons found mostly in Magaha era, in Nalanda particularly, images of Vajrayana Aparajita in which Hindu deities are shown in humiliating manner. I had drawn attention to some of such icons in my address to Indian History Congress Section I in Delhi in 1961, and this has been published (Satakari Mookarji Felicitation volume, pp. 97 ff). All such images belong to 10th century and after, in the heyday of Vajrayana. There is an inscriptional evidence belonging to the 11th year of the reign of Mahipala that the Nalanda University was burnt down and was restored by Baladitya of Taladhake. It is not clear as to who had burnt down the building. An inscription was found in Nalanda which refers to the burning of the Mahavihara by the Vangala army (ASIAR, 1930-34, pp. 212 ff; E.I. XXI, pp. 291ff). Taranatha refers to the burning of Nalanda Tample by the Tirthakas (Brahmin priest). We know that in the south rivalry between the Jains and the Saivas often led to desecration of each other's religious establishments. And as can be gleaned from sculptures on walls of Kailasanatha temple at Kanchipuram, the competitive spirit of the Vaishnava and Saiva movements—Alwars and Nayanars—often led to uprooting of image of one deity by the setting up of the image of the other cult deity. Even in the Puranas we find this scene of one sect claiming superiority over the other's deities and this finds expression in iconography.

Lingodbhava image shows Vishnu and Brahma digging the earth down and surveying over the sky to find the origins of Linga and failing to do so. In the Bhagavada Purana worshippers of Siva are referred as pashandims and opponents of holy scriptures (Bhag. Pu. IV.21). Simultaneously forces of reconciliation were at work. We have Harihara images and the Buddha was accepted as an incarnation of Vishnu.

It is true instances of sectarian violence and humiliation of one by the other sects are very few and far between, but the lesson is, one cannot afford to be complacent. External vigilance is the price of communal peace and religious accord.

It would be naive to believe that religious peace and mutual toleration is the only panacea against disintegration. It is quite obvious today that dangers to national integration come in the form of communalism, linguism, regionalism and communalism, and for each and all of their roots are sought in past history and traditions both for the protagonists and antagonists of national integration. But the sense of unity of the country has been always uppermost in the minds of sages, philosophers, religious prophets, statesmen and great kings. The imperial period of the Mauryas, the Guptas, and the Cholas may be taken as the practical proofs of this strong urge for political unity. The institution of the Vajapeya and Asvamedha sacrifices gave a religious sanction for achieving political unification by military means. The conception of Cakravarti Kshetra, visualised by Kautilya, embracing from the mountains in the north to oceans in the south, east and west as one country—Bharatavarsha—acted as a spur to all the ambitious rulers to be intent on conquest for the realisation of the historic mission of realisation of political unity of India. It is important to note that whenever any king of south or north felt himself strong to make march ahead he did not think of territories outside India's geographical barriers even if it was nearer but only to bring other parts of India under his control. Unity by sword failed to establish permanent unity. The attempt however brilliant proved ephemeral. But this lack of political unity which dominates Indian history for much larger period of time, did not result in the break-up of the country into separate pieces, one having nothing to do with the other. While the kings and the statesmen faded, while the armies could not penetrate into remote corners of the country and could have their hold only temporarily, the philosophers, religious leaders, litterateurs and artists succeeded in keeping up the spirit of oneness or unity of the country, live and real. No religious movement worth mentioning, no philosophy born on the Indian soil, no artistic tradition evolved in the country could remain confined in any religion or among any specific groups of people. The Vedic religion and philosophy, the Vaishnava, Saiva, and Sakti cults, the Buddhist and Jain sects all these arose in one or another part of the country but in course of time overcame the geographical and linguistic barriers and found their way in different nooks and corners of the vast country. Leaders of different religious sects and philosophers soon came to belong to the entire country. Every religion has its holy places spread over through-out the country and has its saints and prophets born in different parts of the country. The distribution of the centres of pilgrimages of different religions in the country forges a strong chain of integration between the inhabitants of different religions. The rich literary and artistic tradition knows no geographical barrier and became common heritage of the entire country. The Epics and the Puranas were and are sources of inspired traditions and beliefs, faiths of entire country. The institution of salutation to Eulaparvatas and great rivers of north and south helped in the growth of the idea of oneness of the great country. The community of religious and mythological ideas and beliefs, the universality of social norms and structure, the common pride in the glorious events and in heroes of the hoary past, and the highly assimilative and synthetic character of the Indian culture as a whole bound the peoples of different religions, speaking different languages and worshipping different gods in such interlinking chains that cannot easily fall asunder. Even in the periods when India was politically divided, the unity of India was inviolable because in those days religious and cultural ties, overstepping the bounds of geographical and linguistic and even political barrier, were far more stronger for unity than the disintegrating political power. Politically divided India was even in the many epochs of political disintegration culturally and fundamentally united in the midst of amazing cultural and religious varieties. In a way the very fact or varieties in Indian cultural and religious life explain the persistence of the sense of fundamental unity of India. Unity in diversity is the refrain in the long Indian cultural history.

India is politically united today. But dangers to this unity from within are mainly from communalism, linguistic chauvinism, desperate economic scenes, and above all regionalism. A student of Indian history should be optimistic about the country overcoming the obstacles. Uniform political system, all-India administrative structure, expansion of communications are some of the factors which were not available in earlier times and these have strengthened the unity of political fabric. But any attempt to be too assertive of political power, too much emphasis on the same uniformity of economy, and to project what is called a dominant culture from commanding heights looking down on regional sub-cultural zones would prove disastrous. That would be rejection of old values of toleration and coexistence of big and small developed and less developed. Old values of life are in the process of being overwhelmed by newer values born of the industrial and technological revolution which impose *uniformity*. But a country like India with rich historical traditions and spiritual values will become much poorer and essentially weaker if ancient values are bid goodbye. We will ignore the lessons of our history at our peril. Vigorous and purposeful efforts are to be made to reinstate the abiding and universal values of historical and cultural traditions to re-awaken or re-enliven the old spirit of 'Samavaya eva Sadhu' to ensure national integration and growth.

In our opinion, the nation in the present predicament of ethnic and religious conflicts should learn from its ancient history. Both the government and the people could profitably adopt Asokan model of concord between communities enjoying full freedom of worship and enforcing among themselves essentials of all religions.